Brian Hayden

111 Places
in Buffalo
That You Must
Not Miss

Photographs by Jesse Pitzler

T0244089

emons:

For my parents, who instilled in me
a love for our region.

© Emons Verlag GmbH
All rights reserved
© Photographs by Jesse Pitzler except see p. 237
© Cover icon: shutterstock.com/Mark_Kostich
Layout: Editorial Design & Art Direction, Conny Laue,
based on a design by Lübbeke | Naumann | Thoben
Maps: altancicek.design, www.altancicek.de
Basic cartographical information from Openstreetmap,
© OpenStreetMap-Mitwirkende, OdbL
Editing: Karen E. Seiger
Printing and binding: Grafisches Centrum Cuno, Calbe
Printed in Germany 2023
ISBN 978-3-7408-2151-7
Revised second edition, October 2023

Guidebooks for Locals & Experienced Travelers
Join us in uncovering new places around the world at
www.111places.com

Foreword

It's hard to remember a time in my life when I wasn't fascinated by my hometown. As a boy, I took sunset walks with my family at Erie Basin Marina on summer evenings, marveling, with an ice cream cone in hand, at the city's skyline, its waterfront, and the Great Lake that stretched into the horizon. When I was in third grade, I even accompanied my dad to Tops Supermarket for an autographed photo of the city skyline by then Mayor Anthony Masiello, who signed the picture, "Dear Brian, Believe in Buffalo… and TOPS!"

Perhaps deep family roots inspired this enthusiasm. Buffalo is where my great-great grandfather owned the city's longest-operating tavern, then known as Dobmeier's, back when the neighborhood was an enclave for German immigrants in the 1890s. This city is also where my grandfather patrolled the streets as a cop, and where my mother and father decided to stay and raise their children, even though many Buffalonians back then believed the city's best days were over.

They weren't, thankfully. I've been fortunate to live here and build a career during a time when new life returned to the city's waterfront, when visionaries reimagined the city's architectural landmarks, and when waves of immigrants from around the world reinvigorated Buffalo's neighborhoods. This book is a tribute to the places and people that shaped Buffalo's past – both its triumphs and tragedies – as well as the trailblazers, entrepreneurs, and creative types building a brighter future for this ever-resilient city and region.

What began as a daunting task – identifying 111 places for this book – turned into a journey of uncovering backstories and developing a deeper appreciation of Buffalo and Niagara Falls that I never want to stop. I hope this book is just the beginning of your own adventure to get to know this remarkable place in a deeper and more meaningful way. Happy exploring!

111 Places

1 Adam Mickiewicz Library

Preserving Buffalo's proud Polish past

Only one place in Buffalo – or likely anywhere, for that matter – boasts a Polish language library, century-old bar and avant-garde theater all under one roof. The Adam Mickiewicz Library and Dramatic Circle has been a mainstay in Buffalo's Broadway-Fillmore neighborhood since 1896, proudly flying its red and white Polish flag outside its front door every Friday evening to invite visitors inside.

At its backroom bar, adorned with pink wallpaper, longtime members sit and chat over shots of Krupnik and cold bottles of Zywiec, Tyskie, and Okocim beer. Upstairs, a sign on a door reading *Biblioteka* guides guests into the library, which holds several thousand Polish-language books about the Eastern European country's geography, history, religion, and culture, and even manuscripts of plays written by members through the generations. At the back of the building, the old auditorium where members performed those plays has been renovated into a state-of-the art black box theater, the home venue of Buffalo's avant-garde Torn Space Theater Company.

The library traces its origins back to when Polish immigrants began settling the city's far East side. They named their neighborhood streets Paderewski, Sobieski, and Kosciuszko, built towering churches like St. Stanislaus and Corpus Christi for Sunday worship, and shopped for pierogi and kielbasa at the Broadway Market. But they needed a place where they could preserve their culture and memories from the Old World for generations to come, so they founded a club and library named after Mickiewicz, a famed Polish poet and playwright.

Even as the once tight-knit Polish neighborhood dispersed and moved out into the suburbs, the Mickiewicz endured. The library opened its doors to members and non-members alike and welcomed Torn Space as a creative partner to ensure it will remain in Buffalo for another 130 plus years.

Address 612 Fillmore Avenue, Buffalo, NY 14212, +1 (716) 847-0839, www.facebook.com/
AdamMickiewiczLibraryandDramaticCircle, amldc1895@gmail.com | Getting there
Bus 23 to Fillmore Avenue & Paderewski Drive | Hours Fri 8pm–2am | Tip Visit the Eugene
V. Debs Social Hall, a socialist-inspired club in the neighborhood that opened in 2021 inside
a restored historic tavern (483 Peckham Street, www.facebook.com/EugeneVDebsHall).

2 — Alethea's Chocolates
Bite into generations of confectionery traditions

When you bite into a piece of Alethea's chocolate, you're tasting a family confectionery tradition that dates back centuries to a small town in Greece. Alethea's Chocolates might just be Buffalo's capital of sweets, boasting more than 300 products lining its shelves and an ice cream parlor that offers all homemade sauces atop your sundae.

Visitors enjoying the sugary fragrances as they peruse the shop will find chocolate-covered malt balls, milk and dark chocolate wafers, chocolate fudge, chocolate-covered potato chips, handmade truffles, and "Charlie Chaplins," a concoction of cashews, coconut, and marshmallow covered in – you guessed it – chocolate. The top seller here is sponge candy: pieces of milk or dark chocolate covering a sugary, crispy center. Buffalo is the epicenter of what Alethea's owner Dean Tassy likes to call the "Sponge Belt," an area stretching from Syracuse to Erie, Pennsylvania, which has sold the candy since the early 20th century. "The rest of the country has tried. In New England, they call it crackle – doesn't cut it. Down South, they call it fairy food – doesn't cut it," Tassy said. "They just don't have the expertise and climatic conditions."

In the production facility behind the store, staff hand-etch the letter A into every piece of fresh sponge candy in honor of Tassy's great-grandmother Alethea, who sold jellies and other confections from her house in Kozani, Greece. Her descendants found their way to Buffalo, part of a wave of Greek families who entered the candy-making business because they knew it was recession-proof, Tassy said. His father Gust purchased the Garden of Sweets, a Bailey Avenue shop owned by another Greek family, in the 1960s and renamed it after Alethea. Generations of the Tassy family and veteran employees have spent decades perfecting their products to make life in Buffalo just a little bit sweeter.

Address 8301 Main Street, Buffalo, NY 14221, +1 (716) 633-8620, https://www.aletheas.com, chocolates@aletheas.com | **Getting there** Bus 47 to Transit Road & Main Street, walk 10 minutes | **Hours** Daily 10am–9pm | **Tip** Also visit Parkside Candy's magnificently restored Art Deco candy shop and ice cream parlor, which dates back to 1927 (3208 Main Street, www.parksidecandy.com).

3 Allentown's Bubble Machine

Bubbly tribute to a neighborhood legend

Every now and then, hundreds of bubbles fill the air above Elmwood Avenue and Allen Street – a lasting reminder of one man's mission to make his neighborhood whimsical. These days, the bubbles originate from a machine outside an apartment window a few floors above the Jim's Steakout restaurant at that corner. But for nearly 40 years, they came from Allentown resident Chuck Incorvaia, who blew bubbles from his window day and night, through sun, wind, and snow, onto the street below until his death in 2022 at the age of 75.

The bubbles drifted from Incorvaia's window, floated above the traffic light, and over the heads of residents walking to the street's many pubs and restaurants. Incorvaia's bubbles were "random and delightful" and "without any agenda, without any purpose beyond joy in the moment," Allentown Association President Patty Macdonald said. "You'd look up for a minute, and your heart would just lift … that corner will forever be the corner where the bubble man was."

Incorvaia used just a bubble wand and a window fan for his decades-long hobby that started after he moved into the apartment in the 1980s. He was a disabled veteran who found that blowing bubbles lifted his spirits as well as everyone else's in the neighborhood, Macdonald said. A nearby neighbor installed the machine on the building's exterior soon after Incorvaia's death and frequently turns it on so that bubbles continue to fill the air after his passing.

Perhaps no other part of Buffalo would have welcomed Incorvaia's bubbles quite like Allentown, the city's long-standing Bohemian enclave filled with rainbow-colored sidewalks, wall murals, art galleries, and live music venues. The Allentown Association is drawing up plans for a more permanent memorial to its beloved "bubble man."

Address Elmwood & Allen Streets, Buffalo, NY 14201 | Getting there Bus 19, 20 to Elmwood & Allen Streets | Hours Unrestricted | Tip Continue your tour of Allentown by catching a show at the PAUSA Art House, a jazz bar run by Cuban-born violinist Lázara Martinez (19 Wadsworth Street, www.pausaarthouse.com).

4 The Ararat Stone

The cornerstone of a Jewish colony that never was

Of all the Buffalo History Museum's thousands of artifacts, perhaps none is as unusual as the 400-pound cornerstone commemorating the Jewish colony on Grand Island that never came to be.

The Ararat Stone rests on the floor inside the museum's exhibit celebrating Erie County's bicentennial. The massive slab of marble represents the failed dream of Mordecai Manuel Noah, a newspaper editor from New York City who proposed a "City of Refuge for the Jews" on several thousand acres of Grand Island in 1825. Under Noah's plan, Jewish US citizens would contribute one piece of gold per year to build and sustain the colony.

He purchased the cornerstone from a marble yard in Cleveland and celebrated its arrival on September 2, 1825 at St. Paul's Episcopal Church in downtown Buffalo and not on Grand Island, as the website mappingararat.com notes, because of a lack of adequate transportation to ship it there. *Hear oh Israel, the Lord our God, the Lord is one*, the Hebrew on the stone reads. But Noah's idea never materialized past the cornerstone, as other Jewish leaders criticized the idea of a colony. The stone remained in a yard behind the church and then found its way to a variety of locations in Buffalo and on Grand Island before ultimately landing at the Buffalo and Erie County Historical Society in 1866. On the far-eastern end of Grand Island, a small roadside plaque near a cemetery commemorates the colony's planned location along East River Road.

There are plenty of other artifacts to see in this beautiful museum along Delaware Park, the only remaining building from Buffalo's 1901 Pan-American Exposition. But as one of the museum's longest held items, the cornerstone stands apart as a poignant reminder of Noah's ambitious plans for the region, and of the promise of religious freedom that the United States came to symbolize as a young country nearly two centuries ago.

Address One Museum Court, Buffalo, NY 14216, +1 (716) 873-9644, www.buffalohistory.org |
Getting there Bus 20 to Elmwood Avenue & Nottingham Terrace | Hours Wed 10am–8pm,
Thu–Sat 10am–5pm, Sun noon–5pm | Tip Discover more Jewish history inside the Benjamin and
Dr. Edgar R. Cofeld Judaic Museum within Temple Beth Zion (805 Delaware Avenue, www.tbz.org).

5 Art's Cafe

A community's transformation through creativity

Along Main Street in Springville, hundreds of community members banded together to save a decrepit and long-vacant building and transform it into a creative hub and village gathering place. Spread across its four floors, Art's Cafe hosts an art gallery, performance stage, bakery, café, maker space, rooftop garden, and a reading room filled with hundreds of books.

On any given day, the café might host an evening of live jazz, a watercolor class, an opening for a local artist, Spanish language lessons, and book binding and stained-glass workshops. The aroma of freshly baked bread fills the bakery, which offers a limited menu of scratch-made soups and sandwiches and sources many of its ingredients from the publicly accessible rooftop garden two floors above. Art's has reinvigorated this brick 19th-century building and infused new energy into downtown Springville. "Something that held so many memories for generations of people in Springville has been brought back to life," worker-owner Allison Duwe said. "It's making new memories for people and will be a positive force in this community for a long time to come."

Duwe grew up in Springville and recalled when the structure previously housed longtime village businesses, like Vander Meer's Bakery and Teddy's Candy Kitchen. But by a decade ago, the building had sat empty for years, and the roof had collapsed into the basement, destroying its interior. A fundraising effort led by the Springville Center for the Arts raised $30,000 in 30 days and helped secure state and federal grants to save and repurpose the building.

With the financial support of more than 200 community owners, the café gradually opened over the course of the COVID-19 pandemic. Art's is a symbol of Springville's resilience and provides yet another reason for you to stop and explore this charming yet often overlooked small town.

Address 5 E Main Street, Springville, NY 14141, +1 (716) 592-9036, www.artscafespringville.com, artscafespringville@gmail.com | Getting there By car, take US 219 S to NY-39 E | Hours Wed–Fri 9am–8pm, Sat 9am–4pm | Tip Attend a concert or a show inside the Springville Center for the Arts, which has brought new life to a former Baptist Church first built in 1869 (37 N Buffalo Street, Springville, www.springvillearts.org).

6 The Assassination Boulder

Marking the spot where a president was shot

Along the grassy median of a quiet residential street, a bronze plaque fixed upon a memorial boulder marks the spot where an assassin's bullet changed the course of American history.

In the Pan-American Temple of Music which covered this spot, President McKinley was fatally shot Sept. 6, 1901, reads the plaque, surrounded on either side by a miniature American flag. None of the charming bungalows and century-old homes surrounding the plaque on Fordham Drive existed in 1901. Back then, these grounds hosted the Pan-American Exposition, a fair that brought tens of thousands of visitors to Buffalo to celebrate the triumphs of the Western World. Wide promenades filled with ornate, Spanish Renaissance-style buildings greeted visitors from around the world.

The fair even attracted President William McKinley, who greeted visitors at the expo's Temple of Music. Anarchist Leon Czolgosz, his bandaged hand concealing a gun, was waiting for the president there. Inside a Delaware Avenue residence, McKinley held on for several days while being treated before finally succumbing to an infection. Czolgosz was tried in a downtown courtroom, which you can still see today in Erie County Hall, and sentenced to death.

McKinley's assassination marred what was intended to be Buffalo's pinnacle year and tarnished the legacy of the exposition. The city ultimately demolished nearly all of the exposition grounds in the following months, and a new neighborhood emerged just north of Delaware Park. Dignitaries gathered in 1921 along Fordham Drive to place the boulder that marked the spot of McKinley's shooting. "In the death of President McKinley, apart from the national loss, a sad, but a noble duty fell to Buffalonians for all times," Buffalo's City Parks Commissioner John F. Malone told the *Buffalo Morning Express* at the unveiling. "We, in a particular manner, will revere his memory."

Address 30 Fordham Drive, Buffalo, NY 14216 | Getting there Bus 5, 20, 32 to Elmwood & Chatham Avenues | Hours Unrestricted | Tip Pay your respects to the fallen president at the McKinley Monument, a 96-foot-tall marble obelisk built several years after the assassination (5 Niagara Square).

7 Assembly House 150

Bringing back the lost trades

Inside a cavernous former Catholic church, a chorus of power tools and the smell of sawdust fill the onetime worship space that has become Assembly House 150, a classroom for Buffalo's next generation of tradespeople.

Where parishioners once gathered for Sunday Mass at Immaculate Conception Church, aspiring carpenters and tradespeople now develop the skills they need to start a new career in Buffalo. They learn the trades inside the "shop" at the site of the former altar, and then use the rest of the space to try their hand at constructing objects and small microstructures within the old church. Walk down the aisle, and you'll see a wooden "quarter house," partially complete with two floors, a staircase, and furniture. A small library is filled with dozens of books about carpentry – all built by the participants in the Society for the Advancement of the Construction Related Arts (SACRA) program.

Since its inception, SACRA has trained more than 100 Buffalonians with an introduction to the trades. Executive Director and founder Dennis Maher described the space as a "center for urban imagination," which evolves, like cities do, as people build it over time.

Maher first purchased the long-shuttered, former 19th-century church several years ago after it had sat vacant for nearly two decades. The building's roof was in disrepair, and a frozen waterfall was leaking into the west transept. He secured and preserved the structure and then reinvigorated it with the SACRA program, which aims to fill Buffalo with the tradespeople it needs to help refurbish its deteriorating housing stock and revitalize its neighborhoods.

The old church is open for public tours, and it is a piece of living art – a microcosm of the broader change taking place throughout Buffalo as SACRA students start their careers. "In my mind," Maher said, "it's a place that's reflective of the city."

Address 150 Edward Street, Buffalo, NY 14201, +1 (716) 560-8170, www.assemblyhouse150.org, info@assemblyhouse150.org | Getting there Metro Rail to Fountain Plaza, walk 15 minutes; bus 20 to Elmwood Avenue & Virginia Street | Hours Tours by appointment; see website for programs and events | Tip Admire the extraordinary stained glass windows inside nearby Trinity Episcopal Church, which also hosts the headquarters of the Stained Glass Association of America (371 Delaware Avenue, www.trinitybuffalo.org).

8   Babcia's Pierogi
New twists on a Broadway Market favorite

Inside a stand at the Broadway Market, Linda Lund serves what might be the most quintessential Buffalo food of all time: chicken-wing and beef-on-weck-filled pierogi. Lund, a retired hairdresser, harnessed her long-held pierogi passion and opened the stand that serves 18 varieties of pierogi in 2017. Standards like cheese and sauerkraut pierogi are on the menu here – mainstays at this legendary public market that catered to the region's Polish population for generations.

But so are stuffed banana pepper, reuben, breakfast scramble, taco, bacon cheeseburger, potato bacon chive, and a dessert flavor resembling hot apple pie. Lund mixes all the ingredients typically found in chicken wings – including blue cheese and diced celery pieces – into her wing pierogi, and she even sells a "pizza-rogi" modeled after a Buffalo-style pepperoni pizza. She started out preparing more traditional flavors, and she branched out when her non-Polish husband wondered why pierogi "had to be so boring."

For Lund, pierogi and the Broadway Market run in the family. She learned how to make pierogi from her grandmother, or "babcia," who lived around the corner from the market and sold what she made in her house to nearby neighborhood taverns. And her father was a salesman for Camellia Meats, a butcher shop located inside the market for decades. So when Lund decided to open her own business, she chose the place she had frequented with her family as a child because it brought back cherished memories.

"You're giving other families those same memories," she said. "It's really cool to be associated with that kind of strong tradition."

Babcia's has been a hit, selling thousands of pierogi each year in the two weeks leading up to Easter alone. The stand is the embodiment of the market today, as it holds onto tradition while also offering its next generation of customers a variety of new flavors.

Address 999 Broadway, Buffalo, NY 14212, +1 (716) 436-3894, www.babciaspierogi.com, babciaspierogi@aol.com | Getting there Bus 4, 19 to Broadway & Lombard Street | Hours Mon – Sat 9am – 5pm, Sun noon – 5pm | Tip Continue your Broadway Market food tour by purchasing a pound of Polish sausage from Camellia Meats, a Buffalo institution since 1935 (999 Broadway, www.camelliameats.com).

9 The Bird Island Pier

Buffalo's 200-year-old buffer from lake storms

Nowhere else in Buffalo showcases Lake Erie's incredible beauty and remarkable fury better than the Bird Island Pier, the city's two-century-old buffer from wild storms. The pier has a narrow walkway that starts at the southern end of Unity Island and extends for more than a mile before dead-ending near the submerged Bird Island Reef at the eastern edge of Lake Erie.

This path whisks you away from the bustle of the city and the din of the nearby thruway to a quiet, peaceful terminus entirely surrounded by fresh water. Along your route to the lake, you will see the swiftly flowing Niagara River and Canada on one side and the Black Rock Channel on the other. You'll cross underneath the Peace Bridge, passing by fishermen expertly casting their lines into the water.

Yet the final portion of the walkway, which reopened to the public in 2022 after it collapsed into the canal following a 2019 windstorm, is a reminder that some days along the pier are far from tranquil. These violent lake storms were on the mind of Buffalo's earliest settlers, who constructed a timber-and-stone pier in the early 1820s in order to protect the harbor and its ships from destructive weather. The pier's construction also created the Black Rock Channel, a safer alternative for vessels to navigate than the turbulent stretch of the upper Niagara River.

According to a 1987 *Buffalo News* article, the original pier was "too dangerous to attract anyone but dedicated fishermen," and up to four people per year drowned by falling off it. The city rebuilt the pier several times and ultimately converted it into a recreational walkway in the 1980s that included a number of new safety measures. At its best, there aren't many more beautiful places in Buffalo to take a walk than Bird Island Pier. Just be sure to check the weather forecast first to make sure one of those wicked lake storms isn't on the horizon.

Address Foot of West Ferry Street, Buffalo, NY 14213 | Getting there Bus 5, 12, 40 to West Ferry & Niagara Streets | Hours Daily dawn – dusk | Tip Take in another unique view of Buffalo when you walk up the 83 steps of the 76-foot-tall observation tower at the Erie Basin Marina (329 Erie Street).

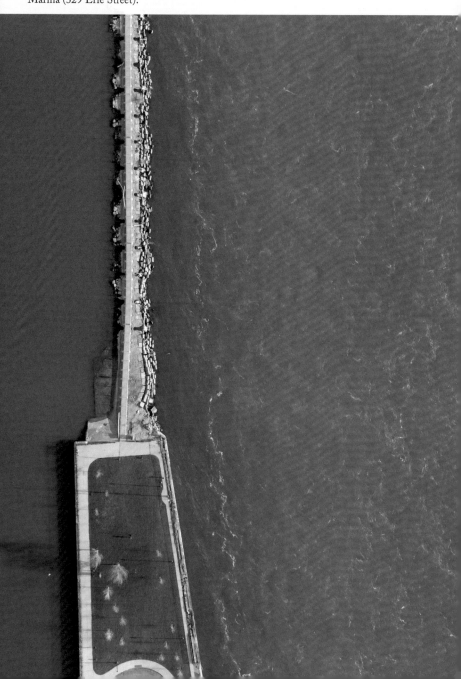

10__The Brain Museums
Study the body's most complex organ – twice

Buffalo's most unusual claim to fame might be that it boasts the country's only *two* museums dedicated exclusively to the study of the human brain. Dozens of preserved brains – some whole, some dissected – rest inside three glass cabinets within a room at the University at Buffalo's (UB) Biomedical Education Building on its South Campus. Downtown, a second Brain Museum at UB's Jacobs School of Medicine displays more than 40 additional specimens.

Between the two exhibits, visitors and students can study more than 100 brains of Buffalonians who donated their bodies to the university for scientific research. There are healthy brains on display and others that show abnormalities: a brain ravaged by Alzheimer's disease, another showing devastation from a stroke, and still others that feature the bulging vessel of an aneurysm and malignant tumors. The South Campus location even features replicas of salmon, hare, dog, and pigeon brains.

UB's late professor of anatomy Dr. Harold Brody introduced Buffalo to its first Brain Museum in 1994, after noticing a display in a hospital while on sabbatical in Denmark. The university added the second museum downtown several years ago after relocating much of its medical school there. The South Campus exhibit boasts the larger collection, while the downtown location is more accessible and also features digital displays. Professor Christopher Cohan, a colleague of Dr. Brody's who has been with the university since 1986, personally provides free tours at both locations. He often brings out a brain for visitors to hold – gloves provided.

Dr. Cohan takes the opportunity to help visitors appreciate the human brain. It's an organ not much bigger than the human fist, but it "is more powerful than anything on this planet," he states. "To me, it's about marveling about how something so small can do so much."

Address Downtown Location: 955 Main Street, Room 111, Buffalo, NY 14203; South Campus Location: 360 Biomedical Education Building, University at Buffalo, South Campus, 3435 Main Street, Buffalo, NY 14203, +1 (716)-829-3081, www.medicine.buffalo.edu, ccohan@buffalo.edu | **Getting there** Metro Rail to Allen/Medical Campus (Downtown Museum) or University (South Campus Museum) | **Hours** By appointment only | **Tip** Discover historic textbooks on nursing, pharmacy, dentistry, and public health inside UB's History of Medicine Collection (B5 Abbott Hall, 3435 Main Street).

11 The Brewster Street Farm
Building community one seed at a time

On two formerly vacant lots east of Main Street, a group of resettled refugee farmers harvest the land at the Brewster Street Farm, just as they did in their home countries across the world. They grow some of the most unique produce found in Western New York on a compact, quarter acre field surrounded by homes on Buffalo's near East Side.

Among rows of crops in these fields and greenhouse, refugees-turned-farmers cultivate bitter gourds often found in Africa, luffa plants usually grown in Asia, Congolese eggplant, and hot chili peppers typically sourced from Bhutan and Nepal. The people who till this soil brought these plant seeds to grow here. They arrive every Thursday morning from spring until fall to collect the week's harvest. They then walk a couple of blocks to the Tri-Main Center, where they sell the day's bounty, which also includes even more traditionally local produce and flowers, at an afternoon farmer's market.

Journey's End Refugee Services started the federally funded farm in 2013 to provide Buffalo's new arrivals with a chance to further develop the farming skills they brought from their homelands. The farm also creates better access to fresh produce for many of these refugee families, who have found their new homes in Buffalo neighborhoods considered "food deserts" for their lack of proximity to fresh fruits and vegetables.

The urban farm, one of a growing number throughout the city, has also reinvigorated a residential street long plagued with vacant properties and better connected the program's participants to the surrounding neighborhood, according to program manager Lauren Dawes. "This neighborhood and the people who work at this farm are a great example of resiliency," Dawes said. "[The farmers] like seeing the fruits of their labor and are very proud of the work they've done here. It's a form of therapy for them and something to take ownership of."

Address 36 Brewster Street, Buffalo, NY 14212, +1 (716) 262-5308, www.jersbuffalo.org/
brewster-street-farm | Getting there Bus 8 to Fillmore Avenue & Jewett Parkway | Hours
By appointment, see website for seasonal farm stand schedule | Tip The West Side Tilth
Farm, another urban farm in Buffalo, makes pizzas topped with farm-fresh veggies on
summer Saturdays (246 Normal Avenue, www.westsidetilth.com).

12 The Buffalo Lighthouse

A beacon for historic preservation

On the edge of the city's waterfront, a nearly two-century-old lighthouse shines bright each night at dusk, a glowing reminder of Buffalo's first successful attempt at historic preservation. The Buffalo Lighthouse is the only building depicted on the city's flag and seal, and it's the oldest structure in Buffalo to remain in its original location.

You can reach the stone tower that first illuminated the harbor back in 1833 by walking a quarter-mile path along a 200-year-old stone breakwater that leads to the confluence of the Buffalo River and Lake Erie. Tours climb the structure's 76 feet by ascending 50 winding stone steps and 3 ladders.

The view from near the top provides spectacular vistas of the city's skyline to the northeast and the limitless expanse of Lake Erie to the southwest. On a windy day, gales from the lake create a deafening roar inside this landmark that helped establish Buffalo as one of the most important ports in America. The grand lens atop this structure guided ships carrying immigrants from the East Coast and freighters hauling in raw materials from the Midwest.

"This was a nexus, a critical juncture, both in human history and in the history of commerce," said Mike Vogel, who has helped maintain the structure for decades.

The lighthouse served the waterfront until 1914, when it was decommissioned. It sat unused for years. The US Army Corps of Engineers suggested destroying the lighthouse in 1961 and submerging the surrounding point to ease ship navigation. That plan sparked a backlash and led to a "Save the Lighthouse" committee that became Buffalo's first preservation success story. The Vogel family then took over the property in the 1980s and re-lit the Fresnel lens for the first time in more than 70 years, ensuring that this remnant of maritime history would serve for generations to come as a beacon for Buffalo.

Address 1 Fuhrmann Boulevard, Buffalo, NY 14203, +1 (716) 264-1707, www.buffalolight.org, buffalolightshines@gmail.com | Getting there By car, take Route 5 W to Fuhrmann Boulevard | Hours Contact for seasonal hours and tours | Tip Learn more about Buffalo's rich maritime history at the Buffalo Harbor Museum, which features models of Great Lakes freighters, historical images, and more (66 Erie Street, www.llmhs.org).

13 Buffalo Shopcraft
Where everything is #MadeinBUF

Of all the gift shops around the city that sell Buffalo-themed trinkets, wall art, and home goods, only one has merchandise exclusively made by local artisans. In an 800-square-foot storefront in the heart of the Elmwood Village, Buffalo Shopcraft features more than 10,000 items created by more than 120 local makers.

This boutique is a one-stop shop for chicken wing and blue cheese-themed refrigerator magnets, table coasters imprinted with the city skyline, bison-shaped earring studs and garden stakes, sponge candy-flavored lip balm, loganberry scented candles, and necklaces that feature the BUF airport code. Even the stationery cards have a buffalo theme, with one illustration depicting Fred Rogers, of *Mister Rogers Neighborhood*, wearing a Buffalo Bills jacket in the City of Good Neighbors. Every holiday season, the store stocks up on beef-on-weck and pierogi-shaped ornaments. And decorative butter lambs with the tagline, *It's Butter in Buffalo* adorn the front of T-shirts and onesies.

A store like this wouldn't have been possible a generation ago, according to owner Christa Penner. The shop is a reflection of the rise of locally made goods that build off the city's manufacturing legacy and the growing level of pride locals and expats have in Buffalo. "We're real scrappy here and we're real proud of it," Penner said. "Now that Buffalo is on the upswing, I think people are even more proud of being part of its growth and its comeback."

Penner first opened Shopcraft as a vendor within another Buffalo-themed gift shop, Thin Ice, before moving into her own standalone location in 2019. Each artisan selling at Shopcraft has to live within 90 miles of Buffalo, which guarantees that revenue from every sale stays right in Western New York. So you can wear your butter lamb T-shirt with pride, knowing your money will be reinvested into the region that you love.

Address 773 Elmwood Avenue, Buffalo, NY 14222, +1 (716) 882-0306, https://buffaloshopcraft.com, hello@buffaloshopraft.com | **Getting there** Bus 20 to Elmwood & Auburn Avenues | **Hours** Tue–Fri 11am–7pm, Sat 10am–7pm, Sun 11am–6pm | **Tip** Walk around the corner to what may be Buffalo's smallest store, The Farm Shop, which sells yogurt and other products made at Blue Hill Farm in East Otto, NY (235B Lexington Avenue, www.buffalofarmshop.com).

14 Buffalo Zoo Bison

Where buffalo definitely roam

In the back corner of The Buffalo Zoo, visitors can see the only live buffalo in the city, an animal that may or might not have ever lived here in the wild. North American Bison have roamed the grounds of the nation's third-oldest zoo since its earliest days nearly 150 years ago. Guests walk past hundreds of other animals – from polar bears and elephants to mountain goats and gorillas – to reach the three bison in their pen, which is the only habitat that faces outwards towards neighboring Delaware Park. Sadly, 30-year-old Wilma died in early 2023.

The zoo's first bison in the late 19th century openly grazed with sheep and elk in the park's meadow and helped to mow its lawn. The current exhibit's design, which allows the bison to look out onto the grassy, expansive golf course just beyond the zoo, pays tribute to this connection to the park – and to the city's love for them. "They're incredibly powerful and strong animals. Their coat is so hearty. And they do very well in harsh conditions," zoo spokesperson Christian Dobosiewicz said. "That's very symbolic of the people of Buffalo."

The beasts may be beloved, but historians have long debated whether bison actually roamed here before the zoo. Researchers at The Buffalo History Museum compiled seven possible theories about Buffalo's name origin. Maybe the city derived its name from Buffalo Creek, but the creek's history is less certain. It's possible, but not likely, that bison did once live here. A phrase the Senecas used to describe the area, meaning "Place of the Basswoods," may have been mistranslated as Buffalo. Or the Senecas may have named the creek after a man called Buffalo. Widely debunked but still popular is that French settlers named the city after the phrase "beau fleuve," or "beautiful river." Whatever the truth may be, the resilient animal eventually came to symbolize the city, and this exhibit at the zoo is the perfect way to honor them.

Address 300 Parkside Avenue, Buffalo, NY 14214, +1 (716) 837-3900, www.buffalozoo.org | Getting there Bus 32 to Amherst Street & Parkside Avenue | Hours See website for seasonal hours | Tip Continue your bison tour by grabbing a selfie with the colorful and whimsical *Magic Buffalo* mural by Bunnie Reiss, which is painted on the back wall of Joe's Deli (1322 Hertel Avenue).

15__Buffalo's Oldest Tree

Centuries-old sycamore has serious competition

Buffalo's quest to determine its oldest tree has created a debate with roots older than the city itself. Just a few blocks north of downtown, a massive sycamore tree leans over Franklin Street. Its roots have caused the surrounding sidewalk to bulge, and its boughs provide ample shade over the street, nearly touching the stately brick house on the other side. *This Sycamore Tree is Believed to be the Oldest Tree in Buffalo, about 250 Years Old,* reads a plaque on its trunk installed in 1960 by the Buffalo Lumber Exchange.

A 1942 *Buffalo Evening News* article details how 17-year-old Charles R. Throm won a $15 Boy Scout contest for discovering that the sycamore was the oldest tree in Buffalo. The *News* described the tree at the time as 78 feet high and 4.5 feet in diameter. A photo accompanying the story shows a proud Throm embracing the tree, his arms only able to make it halfway around the trunk.

But the Lumber Exchange's decision to memorialize Throm's discovery with an official plaque began a broader debate that still hasn't been settled. A *News* column from the early 1980s alleged that the Lumber Exchange installed the plaque without verifying the information and claimed that the sycamore was only the second-oldest tree in Buffalo. An iconic oak inside Buffalo's Delaware Park meadow was five years its senior, the city's chief forester Edwin Drabek told the paper. Another 1935 *Courier-Express* article reported that a great white oak inside Forest Lawn Cemetery may have been even older.

Yet no one seems to argue that the Franklin Street sycamore is the city's largest tree. An underground creek has helped nurture it for centuries, and city crews have tended to it in recent decades to ensure its survival. Oldest or not, the massive sycamore inspires a sense of wonder among all who see it as one of the only trees that was here before European settlers arrived.

Address 402 Franklin Street, Buffalo, NY 14202 | **Getting there** Bus 11, 25 to Delaware Avenue & Edward Street, then walk east on Edward and turn left on Franklin Street | **Hours** Unrestricted | **Tip** See the large oak that vies for competition with the Franklin Street tree inside the Delaware Park meadow (84 Parkside Avenue, www.bfloparks.org/parks/delaware-park).

16 Burnt Ship Creek

Home to sunken ships – and buried treasure?

Grand Island's small, winding Burnt Ship Creek might hold a 260-year-old secret: the sunken ruins of two French ships filled with buried treasure. It's hard to imagine now, but Buckhorn Island State Park's 895 acres of forest, trails, and marsh at the northwestern tip of Grand Island were once in the crosshairs of the French and Indian War. The French burned two ships in the bay at the end of the creek that runs through the present-day state park in the 1750s to avoid capture by the British, according to the 1884 book *The History of Buffalo and Erie County*. "In very low water, the timber heads of one of these vessels may be seen a few inches above the surface," noted H. P. Smith, the book's author.

But does Burnt Ship Bay hold more than just ships? Legend has it that these vessels had treasure on board when the French sent them to the bottom of the river. An 1888 storm lowered the water levels and "revealed gold and silver coins there," according to a 1967 *Buffalo Magazine* article. "One was dated 1537 and coins of later dates were found nearby, and two French frigates were alleged to have been scuttled nearby, one with a pay chest on it." There's even Burnt Ship Bay Winery in Southern Ontario named after the "final resting place for some treasure-laden French ships."

Before you strap on scuba gear and dive into the Niagara's swiftly flowing waters, it's worth noting that no one has written about seeing even the ship's ruins in generations. Treasure or not, a walk along this state park's scenic trail that leads from the Eagle Overlook Parking Lot on West River Road through the forest to a creek overlook is worth it, even if only to imagine the area as a battleground for two world powers struggling for domination nearly three centuries ago. And maybe – just maybe – you'll make a discovery of your own that will add to the lore of Burnt Ship Creek.

Address 5 West River Parkway, Grand Island, NY 14072, +1 (716) 773-3271, www.parks.ny.gov/parks/buckhornisland | Getting there By car, take West River Road to Eagle Overlook Parking Lot | Hours Daily dawn–dusk | Tip Discover more Grand Island history, including stories of President Grover Cleveland's adventures here, at the River Lea house inside Beaver Island State Park (2136 West Oakfield Road, Grand Island, www.parks.ny.gov/parks/beaverisland).

17 The Canalside Ruins
Explore the remnants of the "Infected District"

Along the Commercial Slip at Canalside, visitors can explore a crumbling pile of ruins that serve as the only reminder in this family-friendly district of the waterfront's bad old days.

Today's Canalside features a buzzing collection of attractions and activities along a boardwalk lining the Buffalo River and the Erie Canal's western terminus. But just off the beaten path from there, a series of deteriorating and interconnected stone and brick foundations provide a glimpse into just how different this area once was. Visitors can walk down a ramp from Lloyd Street to the ruins, which feature wooden plank floors and stone walls several feet high. A historical marker notes that the ruin housed Gillet & Sons, a 19th-century producer of heavy-duty high wines and rectified spirits that were popular in the surrounding "hard drinking" neighborhood where the Erie Canal emptied into the Buffalo harbor. *Drinking was common among the people living and working in the Canal District*, the marker noted.

Throngs of sailors and longshoremen once filled the streets surrounding the ruins, which teemed with debauchery. An 1893 Christian Homestead Association map counted 75 "houses of ill-fame" and 108 saloons within several city blocks. Newspapers of the day called it the "infected district," and its central thoroughfare, Canal Street, the "wickedest street in the world," where cops dared not venture alone. A 2011 *Daily Beast* article even speculated that the "dive bar" may have originated at Dug's Dive, a popular neighborhood watering hole at that time.

Buffalo razed the area by the mid-20th century, turning this district of vice into a faded memory. Fortunately, a preservationist-led effort unearthed the ruins in recent years and incorporated them into Canalside, ensuring that future generations will better understand the dark underside of the city's rich waterfront history.

Address Lloyd Street near Prime Street, Buffalo, NY 14202 | Getting there Metro Rail to Erie Canal Harbor, then turn right on Marine Drive and left on Lloyd Street | Hours Unrestricted | Tip Wander over to the nearby Queen City Bike Ferry for a $1 ride across the Buffalo River to the miles of lakeshore hiking and biking trails along the Outer Harbor (44 Prime Street, www.queencityferry.com).

18 Central Terminal Clock
The secret of the train station's meeting spot

Generations of Buffalonians walked past the 14-foot, cast-iron Central Terminal clock on their way to catch a train without knowing that the station centerpiece served a secret purpose.

The cavernous, 550,000-square-foot train station could handle up to 250 trains and 3,000 passengers per day when it first opened in 1929. The clock served as a gathering place within the station, where passengers often looked for their loved ones after a long train ride. "When you came into this building, you were told, 'Meet me at the clock,'" longtime volunteer Marty Slawiak said. "This is where you met your sweetheart. This is where you met your ride back from the service."

But the ticking landmark had a whole different purpose for the New York Central Railroad police. When cops knew of a criminal being transferred by train to a new jail, they notified the staff working the information desk by the clock. That station employee would quietly turn on the green light on top of the clock, which alerted the soda shop, shoeshine stand, Union News Company, and other merchants along the concourse that a high-risk security threat had entered the building and to be on guard. The small bulb flickered off once the security threat cleared the concourse.

Time eventually ran out for the clock – and for passenger services at the Central Terminal, with the last Amtrak locomotive departing the station in 1979. By the 1990s, much of the station's ornamentation had been removed and sold for scrap. The clock eventually wound up in a salvage yard in Chicago. Happily, in 2009, the Central Terminal Restoration Corporation partnered with M&T Bank to bring the clock back to Buffalo, restore it to its original grandeur, and re-install it in its original location. Today, the clock and its green bulb shine bright once again – a symbol of the resurgence of this architectural landmark – and of Buffalo itself.

Address 495 Paderewski Drive, Buffalo, NY 14212, +1 (716) 754-6142,
www.buffalocentralterminal.org, info@buffalocentralterminal.org | Getting there Bus 23 to Fillmore
Avenue & Paderewski Drive, walk six blocks east | Hours See website for seasonal tours and events |
Tip Discover a miniature world of model locomotives in Hamburg at one of the last independently
owned model train hobby shops in the area, Artcraft Toy Trains (4 Scott Street, Hamburg).

19__Charles Burchfield Studio
The workspace of an American master

Charles Burchfield created some of the country's most iconic water-color paintings from the humblest of spaces. His backyard studio in West Seneca is now on display at the Burchfield Penney Art Center. The artist built the 14-by-17-foot studio behind his house on Clinton Street to separate himself from the "family noises" that made it "impossible to concentrate when the children are quarreling or yelling," he wrote to a friend in 1928. In this space, he spent countless hours creating hundreds of watercolor landscapes that eventually garnered him national acclaim until his death in 1967.

The recreated studio features much of its original furniture and decor, from his rocking chair and taxidermy birds lining the walls to shelving units filled with works in progress and his easel and brushes. Other items reflect his deep interest in nature, including pinecones and tree bark sitting on a counter, and a turtle back rock lugged in from a hiking excursion. Burchfield often ventured to Cazenovia Creek across the street from his house and other nearby forests to find inspiration for his paintings.

The studio's linoleum floors and unassuming furnishings strike a chord with visitors. "He lived in a very modest home in a very modest neighborhood. He never was hugely rich, but his richness came from experience," said Nancy Weekly, the center's head of collections. "I think it's just relatable, especially for students thinking about what they can do within their own means."

Following Burchfield's death, his next-door neighbor purchased the property and donated most of the studio's contents to the center, where it spent decades in storage. The center, which displays a rotating collection of Burchfield's works, debuted the rebuilt studio in 1998. This is one of the only places to see the recreated space where an American master perfected his craft.

Address 1300 Elmwood Avenue, Buffalo, NY 14222, +1 (716) 878-6011, www.burchfieldpenney.org, burchfld@buffalostate.edu | Getting there Bus 20 to Elmwood Avenue & Rockwell Road | Hours Wed, Fri, & Sat 10am–5pm, Thu 10am–8pm, Sun 1–5pm | Tip Retrace Burchfield's steps along the trails of the Charles E. Burchfield Nature & Art Center, which runs along Buffalo Creek in Gardenville, near where the artist lived (2001 Union Road, West Seneca, www.burchfieldnac.org).

20__ Common Council Chamber

Inspired by ancient civilizations

Buffalo has one of the only City Halls in the country with a magnificent common council chamber modeled after the amphitheaters of ancient Greece and Rome. You can visit the chamber yourself during regularly scheduled Common Council meetings.

The 13th-floor chamber inside this Art Deco masterpiece is as much of a work of art as it is a room for governance. In every corner of the room, architect John Wade seems to reach out from the past and urge present-day lawmakers to conduct their work as transparently as possible. Hundreds of pieces of stained glass, shaped and colored like the sun, form a skylight above the lawmakers' desks and infuse the entire room with light on a sunny day. The sunburst also features all the planets of the solar system and more distant stars, seemingly suggesting that the eyes of God watch over the city's proceedings. On the wall below the sunburst, are written the words in all-capitalized letters, *PEOPLE'S COUNCILORS REFLECT THE PEOPLE'S WILL.*

Along the pillars lining the room, busts representing the virtues of governance face outward towards the lawmakers, from Concordia and Courage to Prudence and Wisdom, with a long, curly beard.

The seven semicircular rows of wooden stadium seating surrounding the lawmakers ensure excellent acoustics and unobstructed views of the proceedings, just as the ancient amphitheaters once did. Wade had these civilizations on his mind when he constructed the 32-story City Hall, which remains one of the country's largest municipal buildings, at the astronomical cost of $8 million in 1931 dollars. "In the new City Hall, there is the same striving to interpret the life and feeling of the present time that you will find in the monumental buildings of Athens and Rome," he told *The Buffalo Times* in 1931.

Address 65 Niagara Square, Buffalo, NY 14202, +1 (716) 851-4890, www.buffalony.gov/362/ Common-Council | **Getting there** Bus 1, 2, 3, 4, 5, and more to Niagara Square & City Hall | **Hours** Check website for public meeting times | **Tip** For another architectural wonder, walk over to the Ellicott Square Building to gaze down upon the mosaic floor containing 23 million pieces of Italian marble (295 Main Street, www.ellicottdevelopment.com/portfolio/ ellicott-square-building).

21 Colored Musicians Club

Where musical legends have jammed

Some of the biggest names in jazz once jammed at the Colored Musicians Club (CMC). Nearly a century old, this performance space doubles today as a shrine to Buffalo's music history. It's one of the last venues of its kind left in the country.

Generations of Buffalo's most talented musicians have performed inside the brick walls of this club on the edge of downtown. When visitors first walk into the downstairs museum, they'll see a photo from decades ago of Dizzy Gillespie, Miles Davis, and John Coltrane all packed tightly into the upstairs club during an unforgettable night there. CMC members backed up these legends when they performed in Buffalo and then returned to the club afterwards to play with them late into the night. The museum provides sound sticks to sample songs and styles of music played there over the decades, and shares the story of the club's most prominent members through a series of interactive exhibits. Upstairs, the CMC's original wooden bar from 1935 remains intact, and the cozy venue ensures there isn't a bad seat in the house for the jazz still performed there today.

Back when the club first started, racial segregation pervaded Buffalo's music scene. Black musicians founded the Local 533 Union in 1917 to secure more work and built the venue as their home nearly two decades later. The club produced some of the greatest musical talent in Buffalo's history, including saxophonist Grover Washington, Jr., who went on to achieve national acclaim. Club members held onto the venue after the union integrated in the 1960s and then did everything they could to keep the doors open even as Buffalo's jazz heyday faded into memory. They persevered and opened the museum a decade ago, and embarked on a club renovation and expansion scheduled for completion in late 2023. Their hard-fought efforts will help the beat go on here for years to come.

Address 145 Broadway, Buffalo, NY 14203, +1 (716) 855-9383, www.thecoloredmusiciansclub.com, info@thecoloredmusiciansclub.com | Getting there Bus 4, 19 to Broadway & Michigan Avenue | Hours Thu – Sat 11am – 4pm or by appointment (museum); see website for club showtimes | Tip Look for the historical plaque nearby that marks the site of the Little Harlem Hotel, where legends like Cab Calloway once performed and stayed. Fire destroyed the hotel in 1993 (494 Michigan Avenue).

22 Concordia Cemetery

The curse of a grieving mother

Of the 21,000 people buried in Concordia Cemetery on Buffalo's East Side, only one tombstone features a curse in the words of a grieving mother mourning her murdered son. "To he who killed in such a violent way by striking down in such a ghastly manner," the tombstone reads in German, "From deep within my heart, you will be handed over to a higher power for swift judgment. You're wished a curse upon your soul when the time is right."

Those words were likely written by Katherine Schmand, the mother of 17-year-old Louis Schmand, who set out from Buffalo in search of adventure in 1877. He never returned. Louis was found dead a few weeks later in Ohio, brutally beaten with a tree limb and partially buried. His father Charles, a German immigrant who owned a wallpaper business in Buffalo, traveled to Ohio to retrieve the body after reading a story in the *Buffalo Courier* about the murder and realizing that the description matched his son. Louis' murderer was never found, and his homicide was but one of the tragedies to strike Katherine Schmand, who buried six other children and her husband before dying in 1897. All of them are listed on the family headstone.

At Concordia, every stone, like the Schmand family's, tells a story, according to Bonnie Fleischauer of the Concordia Foundation. First-generation German immigrants, one of the earliest groups to settle the city, created the 15-acre cemetery on the far East Side in 1859 as those settlers began to need final resting places. The cemetery recently earned a spot on the National Register of Historic Places because of the ornamentation found on the 19th-century headstones and graves, from small marble lambs marking deceased babies to draped urns that symbolized mourning. "These were not the movers and shakers. These were not the giants of industry," Fleischauer said. "These were the workers of Buffalo who literally built this city."

Address 438 Walden Avenue, Buffalo, NY 14211, +1 (716) 892-2909, www.concordiabuffalo.org, concordia1859@gmail.com | **Getting there** Bus 22 to Walden & Koons Avenues | **Hours** Daily dawn–dusk seasonally | **Tip** Continue your exploration of Buffalo's German immigrant community by ordering a pint at Ulrich's 1868 Tavern, the city's oldest pub (674 Ellicott Street, www.facebook.com/ulrichstavern).

23 Connors Hot Dog Stand
Potatoes in the morning, fries by lunchtime

For a few magical weeks at the end of every summer, Connors Hot Dog Stand along the shores of Lake Erie serves French fries from fresh potatoes grown on a farm just a few miles from the restaurant. Potatoes that are in the ground at dawn on late August and September mornings will become someone's tasty fries by lunchtime. Connors figured out the farm-to-table movement decades before the rest of the world decided it was trendy.

Connors, which has been serving beachgoers and cottage dwellers along Old Lakeshore Road since 1944, has partnered with Chiavetta's Potatoes since the 1950s, back when McDonald's began to popularize French fries and Americans expected them as a part of their fast food meals. The friendship between the Connors and Chiavetta families has gone back generations. An off menu "Vetta burger" is even named after potato farmer Mike Chiavetta, who grew up eating here.

Connors' menu stands apart from other roadside stands in Buffalo. The restaurant serves Wardynski's hot dogs instead of the Sahlen's found elsewhere, Italian sausage from the Lakeside Market down the street, fried bologna sandwiches with onions and cheese, and hand-cut pickles that are a favorite at the toppings bar. Dessert is local favorite Perry's Ice Cream. But the fries are the standout: golden brown, crispy, and lightly salted on the outside, and a perfect pillow of potato on the inside.

With picnic-table seating and wide-open garage door windows designed for the cool Lake Erie breezes from across the street, Connors is the perfect spot for visitors with sand between their toes who stop in after a day at the beach. Much has changed since 1944. The prices advertised on a vintage Connors' menu in the seating area tout ice cream cones for a dime and milkshakes for 30 cents. But the Connors family's commitment to tradition and quality remains the same as it ever was.

Address 8905 Lake Shore Road, Angola, NY 14006, +1 (716) 549-1257, www.connorshotdogstand.com, connorshotdogstand@gmail.com | Getting there By car, take NY-5 W to Lake Street, then left onto Old Lake Shore Road; bus 76 to Old Lake Shore Road & Lake Street | Hours Apr–Sep, Mon–Thu 11am–9pm, Fri & Sat 11am–11pm, Sun 11am–10pm | Tip Bring your hot dogs and fries down the street to Lake Erie Beach Park, which offers the perfect spot for a picturesque sunset picnic along the lake (9568 Lake Shore Road, Angola, www.townofevans.org/departments/parks/lebp.html).

24 Cross Over the Line Rodeo

Saddle up at Alden Community Church

Motorists cruising down US 20 on summer Saturdays pass the largest Christian rodeo in the Eastern United States, or, as Alden Community Church Pastor Matt Gold calls it, "Rubberneck City."

Dozens of cowboys and cowgirls from as far away as Texas converge on the front lawn of this countryside church, their trailers filled with horses and bulls. By 5pm, hundreds of spectators arrive on the bleachers surrounding the outdoor dirt arena with their eyes glued on the rodeo gate flanked with American flags. The crowd roars with approval over the next two hours, as rodeo acts trick ride and barrel race on horseback and hang on to their bucking, 1,800-pound bulls. "Let's see if he can get the job done! Let's get up on our feet for the final man of the night! Let's stand and help this cowboy get to the eight-second whistle!" bellows Louis Backlas, co-owner of Cross Over the Line Rodeo, from his announcer's stand.

The arena is the "field of dreams" for Backlas and his parents Fred and Michelle, who founded Cross Over the Line in nearby Warsaw in 1999 and completed the Alden Community Church facility in 2021. Fred, a native of North Tonawanda, wrangled horses and bulls on the US rodeo circuit for decades before returning to Western New York to start his own company. The family envisioned a rodeo arena for all ages, free of the alcohol and drugs often found elsewhere on the circuit. They found a partner in Pastor Gold, who delivers a Christian message during every event's intermission and staffs the event with church volunteers.

The place to be every summer Saturday, the rodeo is a celebration of the "ranchers of the Northeast," as Louis Backlas calls them, and of a lifestyle still found along the country roads of New York State. The rodeo is a taste of the American West right here in Western New York.

Address 1400 Sullivan Road, Alden, NY 14004, +1 (716) 937-7329, www.instagram.com/crossoverthelinerodeo, crossovertheline777@gmail.com | Getting there By car, take US 20 to Sullivan Road | Hours Jun–Aug, Sat 5–7pm | Tip Top off your Alden road trip with a sundae at Pink Cow Ice Cream, a small stand inside the Tractor Supply Company plaza that features pink and white-colored benches and decor (13119 Broadway, www.facebook.com/pinkcownation).

25_ The Custom Hatter

Buffalo's celebrity hatmaker

From his small shop on Broadway, Gary White has created hats for some of the most iconic stars of that other, more famous Broadway – and Hollywood, for that matter.

White's legacy is all over legendary motion pictures, theater, and television shows from the last 45 years – from Harrison Ford's hat in *Indiana Jones and The Last Crusade*, to Steve Buscemi's fedora in *Boardwalk Empire*, and Jake and Elwood's pork pies in *The Blues Brothers*. This far-east-side store is both an active hat-making shop and a display of autographed celebrity customer photos, including David Letterman, James Earl Jones, and Jack Nicholson, who wore one of White's creations as The Joker in Tim Burton's 1989 *Batman*.

He owns one of the world's largest collections of antique hat-making equipment, which allows him to make headwear just as it was assembled a century ago. When customers first walk into The Custom Hatter, they'll find shelves and tables filled with thousands of hat supplies, but no ready-made headwear for sale. That's because White has custom fitted and made to order every single one of the thousands of hats he created over the last four decades.

White grew up in the neighborhood and chose to remain here even after word began to spread nationwide about his talent and craft. He has spent his entire life around hats, first working as a teenage stockman for the downtown men's store, Peller & Mure, before becoming a retail buyer and learning more about the industry. After completing an apprenticeship in Massachusetts, he launched his own shop in the 1980s and has no plans to slow down anytime soon.

A wall filled with thank you notes reflects his customers' appreciation for his dedication and commitment to quality work. "If you're going to do something, why not be good at it?" White asks. "If you're good at your craft, you'll never work a day in your life."

Address 1318 Broadway, Buffalo, NY 14212, +1 (716) 896-3722, www.custom-hatter.com, thecustomhatter@gmail.com | Getting there Bus 4, 19 to Broadway & Mohr Street | Hours Mon–Fri 8am–5pm and by appointment | Tip Catch a glimpse of a Hollywood movie star as they drive into Buffalo Filmworks, a group of repurposed warehouses that serve as a production studio for major Hollywood movies (370 Babcock Street, www.buffalofilmworks.com).

26 Delaware Park's Mass Grave

Tragic burial ground hiding in plain sight

Golfers, dog-walkers, and city residents out for an afternoon stroll often cross through the Delaware Park meadow with no idea of what – and who – lies beneath. A mass grave for some 300 soldiers has been buried in the heart of this field for more than 200 years – decades before Frederick Law Olmsted even considered turning this land into a public park.

A simple plaque on a stone first dedicated in 1896 and nestled between two willow trees marks the spot of the grave that's situated between the second hole and the third tee of the golf course. It wasn't far from here, in an area known as Flint Hill (close to present-day Canisius College) that scores of soldiers camped out during the War of 1812 as they prepared to invade Canada. Buffalo's winter weather was no match for many of them, and illness ravaged the camp, killing hundreds. Farmers Daniel Chapin and Rowland Cotton buried the deceased in a meadow at Chapin's nearby farm on land that would eventually become Delaware Park. One of Buffalo's nearby parkways bears Chapin's name.

"It's hallowed ground," former Olmsted Parks Conservancy Executive Director Stephanie Crockatt said. "This should remind us that it wasn't so long ago that wars like this were happening right at our border, and people sacrificed their lives."

The gravesite is not easy to find, set back roughly on a triangulation between the tennis courts and the snack bar along Ring Road. But when you venture out to discover it (and remember to keep your eye out for flying golf balls along the way), your reward will be finding one of the most peaceful spots in the city. Perhaps the best season to experience this hidden gem is in winter, when the chilly surroundings remind us of the challenging conditions those soldiers endured here.

Address Delaware Park, Buffalo, NY 14214, +1 (716) 838-1249, www.bfloparks.org/parks/delaware-park | Getting there By car, park at the lot at East Meadow Drive near Parkside Avenue and Route 198. Walk west along the all-pedestrian Ring Road to the tennis courts then into the meadow (golf course) to find the gravesite. | Hours Daily 7am–10pm | Tip A historical plaque by Canisius College marks the spot where the War of 1812 encampment at Flint Hill once stood (Main Street & Humboldt Parkway).

27 Devil's Hole State Park

Where Seneca warriors fought for sovereignty

One of the region's most beautiful hiking spots was also the site of a violent chapter of history: a deadly altercation centuries ago between the British and the Senecas. Generations of Western New York hikers have enjoyed the extraordinary scenery at Devil's Hole State Park along the Niagara Gorge. They descend hundreds of stone steps from the gorge's rim down to a trail that straddles the raging rapids of the Niagara River below.

But long before it was a popular outdoor destination, the Devil's Hole, named for a stretch of challenging terrain along the gorge, was the site of a Seneca ambush in September of 1763, just months after the formal conclusion of the French and Indian War. Dozens of Seneca warriors armed with tomahawks, war clubs, and muskets emerged from the forest. They surrounded a British supply train of wagons traveling along the gorge's rim, and another group of soldiers a short distance away. Some historical records estimate that the Haudenosaunee killed nearly 100 British soldiers in hand-to-hand combat along the brink of the gorge. Many perished as they fell into the chasm below.

The attack reflected a fear among Indigenous leaders that European settlers were bringing their way of life to an end, according to Joe Stahlman, former director of the Seneca Iroquois National Museum. While they preferred peace, many believed action was necessary because of incursions into their sovereignty. "People did conspire, and they really did want to push out the Europeans," Stahlman said. "These are freedom fighters. These are people trying to preserve a way of life. They're not full of venom or hatred."

Visitors to the park today will find little evidence of this deadly event. But hikers should remember as they climb the rocky gorge that this stunningly beautiful site was once a flashpoint in the struggle for survival in North America.

Address Niagara Scenic Parkway, Niagara Falls, NY 14305, +1 (716) 284-5778, www.parks.ny.gov/
parks/42 | **Getting there** By car, take I-190 N to Niagara Scenic Parkway South | **Hours** Unre-
stricted | **Tip** Continue your exploration of history along the Niagara Gorge by stopping by the
Lewiston Mound, an Indigenous burial ground that may predate AD 200, at Earl W. Brydges
Artpark State Park (400 S 4th Street, Lewiston, www.parks.ny.gov/parks/113).

28 Dnipro Cultural Center
Celebrate Ukraine at this social hall

Those who support a free, democratic, and independent Ukraine – no Russian imperialists allowed – have gathered for Friday night fellowship for decades inside a century-old social hall on Buffalo's East Side. Ukrainians and friends of Ukrainians convene over bottles of Obolon lager, feast on steaming bowls of borscht and homemade pierogi prepared by first-generation immigrants, listen to streaming Ukrainian radio stations that play the country's latest pop hits, and watch traditional Ukrainian dance videos on the flatscreen above the bar. For a $20 annual membership, you too can partake in this weekly East-Side tradition. Or get buzzed in at the front door by the bartender, who will sponsor you as a visitor for the evening.

The Dnipro Ukrainian Cultural Center has served as a hub of Buffalo's Ukrainian community since 1955, when thousands of immigrants, lured to the area by the abundance of steel and automotive manufacturing jobs, settled on the city's East Side and sought a new gathering place. They found it inside a former German Orioles Hall from 1914 that featured an old rathskeller that they turned into their lounge, and an ornate auditorium that became their banquet space. Members painted a large Ukrainian flag on the building's exterior and installed a community library filled with Ukrainian-language books. The rathskeller-turned-lounge is the center of activity on Friday nights from Labor Day to Memorial Day, and it serves nearly one dozen different varieties of Ukrainian beer and liquor.

Dnipro spent much of its existence in relative obscurity until the 2022 Russian invasion of Ukraine. The social hall quickly became Buffalo's top gathering place for fundraisers, speakers, and other aid mobilization efforts. Pull up a chair in the lounge on a Friday night and support this warm, welcoming, and hospitable community that has been here for decades.

Address 562 Genesee Street, Buffalo, NY 14204, +1 (716) 202-8804, www.dniprobuffalo.com |
Getting there Bus 18, 24 to Genesee Street & Jefferson Avenue | Hours Fri 6–10pm | Tip
Visit Buffalo's Ukrainian American Cultural Center, another club in Black Rock that dates
back to 1900 (205 Military Road, www.facebook.com/ukiclub).

29   Doris Records

Where Rick James promised big things

Buffalo's oldest record store has influenced the musical tastes of generations of Buffalonians – even one of the city's most famous superstars. More than 60 years have passed since the late Mack Luchey opened the first Doris Records, which he named after a young woman he courted and would eventually marry, on Buffalo's East Side. Luchey attracted customers in those early days by attaching a megaphone to the store's exterior and blasting the latest hits that he picked up in New York City, like Booker T. and the MGs' "Green Onions." Those tunes carried from his East Ferry Street location to the apartment building next door, where a young James Johnson – later known as Rick James – was growing up.

Johnson's mother leased the space next to Doris for her soul food restaurant, and the budding musician frequently spent time in the record store perusing albums and hanging out. The musician promised Luchey that he was going to make it big one day. He wrote down the contact information he found on the back of a record inside the store for music executive Berry Gordy, Jr., who would help launch his career. After James reached superstardom, he still returned to visit Doris Records and Luchey, often with a crowd in tow.

Much has changed since those days at Doris. The soul food restaurant James' mother ran is long gone, as is the apartment building where he grew up. And Doris Records has transitioned from selling records to cassette tapes, CDs, and now records again as tastes have evolved. The East Ferry Street store remains a place to connect with the city's proud music history and discover rare vinyl finds and deep cuts from Stevie Wonder, Richard Pryor, and Marvin Gaye, among the hundreds of records and CDs for sale. "Doris Records has meant a lot to a lot of people over the years," Luchey's son, Derrick said. "I'm so glad to keep the legacy alive."

Address 286 East Ferry Street, Buffalo, NY 14208, +1 (716) 883-2410, dorisrec@aol.com |
Getting there Bus 13, 18 to East Ferry Street & Jefferson Avenue | Hours Mon–Sat 10am–10pm |
Tip Shop for more records at Ishy's Records & Hot Sauce Outlet, which sells hundreds
of bottles of hot sauce alongside a wide vinyl selection (5833 Buffalo Street, Sanborn,
www.facebook.com/DavidNiagaraRecords).

30__The Downtown Bazaar
Feast on flavors from around the world

Perhaps no other culinary experience in Buffalo quite embodies the city's diversity – and its resilience – like the Downtown Bazaar. This new food hall on Main Street features a half-dozen food and clothing vendors whose owners hail from around the world. Chefs from as far away as the Philippines, Ethiopia, and South Sudan prepare *sambusas*, *kofta kebabs*, purple yam ice cream, beef stew and a variety of other indigenous cuisines. Aromas of chicken coated in Filipino barbeque sauce and grilled pork belly blend with generous portions of steamed vegetables placed on top of Ethiopian flatbread. Nearby, merchants sell colorful Sri Lankan dresses, jewelry, and other accessories. Recent immigrants rub shoulders with politicians, college professors, and corporate executives, all brought here by one of Buffalo's most diverse array of foods.

"This represents what Buffalo aspires to be. Diversity can bloom in our city. We can provide the opportunity," said Carolynn Welch, executive director of the Westminster Economic Development Initiative (WEDI). "There's just so much hope in here."

The bazaar offers reduced rent, space, and training to aspiring entrepreneurs, many of whom recently moved to Buffalo from overseas. The concept thrived after WEDI opened its first location more than a decade ago, and dozens of applicants currently await in the pipeline for a space to rent. A tragic 2022 fire closed this location's predecessor, the longstanding West Side Bazaar on Grant Street. But it wouldn't take long for WEDI and its merchants to bounce back, opening a new location inside the former EXPO Food Hall downtown in 2023 after the community banded together to support the organization. WEDI plans to soon open another location on Niagara Street that will add space for more than two dozen vendors, ensuring more opportunity for Buffalo's newest residents than ever before.

Address 617 Main Street, Buffalo, NY 14203, +1 (716) 393-4088, www.wedibuffalo.org/
downtown-bazaar, info@wedi.org | Getting there Metro Rail to Fountain Plaza, walk one
block north | Hours Mon–Fri 8am–8pm | Tip Continue your tour of Buffalo's international
food scene at Freddy J's diner, whose effusive owner, Fred Daniel, hails from Liberia
(195 Grant Street, www.facebook.com/freddyjsongrant).

31 Eden's Kazoo Factory
Birthplace of everyone's favorite instrument

On a rural road 45 minutes south of Buffalo, a small factory has been churning out the only metal kazoos made in the United States for more than a century.

The village of Eden – population 7,500 – has carved out a reputation as the nation's metal kazoo capital. Inside the Kazoo Factory, Museum and Gift Shop of Eden, patrons can explore all things kazoo. Visitors walk within feet of the factory's original belt and pulley system powered by a 10-horsepower electric motor – the same machine that still makes the instrument today – and learn about its storied history. A gift shop up front sells kazoo-themed hats and T-shirts alongside more than 10,000 kazoos made on site each year, including variations shaped like a trombone, trumpet, French horn, and even an ear of corn that honors the town's agricultural roots. The museum also explores the kazoo's evolution, from its long-ago African predecessors to the apparatus most known today.

The factory that put Eden on the map for kazoos didn't even make the instrument that it first opened in 1907. It wasn't until nearly a decade later that a traveling salesman introduced the plant management to the owners of a wooden kazoo factory in Georgia, where the instrument had originated some 70 years earlier. The connection inspired the Eden manufacturer to begin producing a metal kazoo, and demand grew to such an extent that the factory stopped making other goods. The metal kazoo, which many musicians prefer for its clearer, sharper tone, gradually eclipsed its wooden counterpart in popularity.

The not-for-profit Suburban Adult Services Inc. has operated the factory since 2002 and provides developmentally disabled adults with opportunities to learn new skills and generate income. This small-town manufacturer has stood the test of time producing the instrument that creates one of the signature sounds of Western New York.

Address 8703 S Main Street, Eden, NY 14057, +1 (716) 992-3960, www.edenkazoo.com, edenkazoo@gmail.com | Getting there By car, take US 62 S to Eden | Hours Mon–Sat 10am–5pm, closed Jan & Feb; call for tours | Tip Grab a meal of Chiavetta's famous barbeque chicken to-go afterwards at the company's nearby flagship location that dates back to the 1950s (10654 Brant-Angola Road, Brant, www.chiavettas.com).

32___The *Edward M. Cotter*

Climb aboard the oldest active fireboat

For more than a century, the world's oldest working fireboat has docked along the Buffalo waterfront by the Michigan Avenue bridge, ready to spring into action for the next inferno. "They just don't make boats like this anymore," said John Sixt, the captain of the *Edward M. Cotter*. "Whether you're a fireman or not, it's a unique piece of history." Since first arriving in Buffalo in 1900, this vessel has fought countless fires along the river and in the Buffalo harbor, from grain silo explosions to flames shooting off lake freighters.

These days, visitors can call Captain Sixt, who works in the small waterfront fire hall next to the *Cotter*, to arrange a personalized tour of the moored boat. He guides guests down a few short steps from the dock into the *Cotter*'s expansive engine room, through the pilot house with a vintage compass and captain's wheel, and past the galley, complete with a refrigerator from the 1950s. The tour ends on the deck of the vessel, which features several fire turrets that can extinguish a blaze by collectively shooting off 15,000 gallons of water per minute towards their target.

Back when the *Cotter* first arrived here, Buffalo was one of the world's busiest ports, and all the wood-framed warehouses and ships lining the harbor were a tinder box ready to combust. The Buffalo Fire Department has rebuilt this 118-foot-long, 178-ton boat three times since 1900, one of which was necessary because the *Cotter* itself caught fire during a 1928 blaze.

As shipping traffic fell away and industry ceased in the late 20th century, so did the number of fires that the *Cotter* needed to fight. Today, the vessel spends most of its days moored, occasionally heading up the river in winter to break up ice, and setting off on private cruises on idyllic summer evenings. This National Historic Landmark is a proud relic and enduring icon of Buffalo's maritime past.

Address 155 Ohio Street, Buffalo, NY 14203, +1 (716) 846-4265, www.emcotter.com | Getting there Bus 44 to South Park & Michigan Avenues, walk one block south | Hours By appointment only | Tip Rock climb and zip line among the ruins of old grain silos at the nearby Buffalo RiverWorks, the city's repurposed waterfront playground (359 Ganson Street, www.buffaloriverworks.com).

33__The Eternal Flame

A natural wonder that really makes you wonder

At the end of a winding hike up Shale Creek, one of Western New York's greatest natural wonders – and mysteries – comes into view: a flickering flame behind a waterfall.

Small trail markers illustrated with fire lead hikers on the half-mile journey from the parking lot to the Eternal Flame Falls. The trail winds its way through a towering forest before descending a 150-foot gorge into the babbling creek bed below. You'll have to straddle either side of Shale Creek, occasionally hopping over rocks and tree branches, before reaching the final destination. A quick whiff of sulfur from the surrounding shale rock means the flame is close.

Reaching the rushing waterfall only takes 30 minutes at most, but discovering the extraordinary flame, which can reach up to 8 inches in height, feels more like a victory at the end of a daylong quest. It's worth pausing here and finding a good sitting rock to gaze into the fire before making the return trip.

The gas that feeds the flame, a mixture of propane, methane, and ethane, originates from 1,300 feet below the ground, according to county park rangers. But no one knows for sure who – or what – started the fire. Indiana University Professor Arndt Schimmelmann, who has studied such flames around the world, speculated that Indigenous populations may have smelled the gas and first ignited the flame thousands of years ago.

The flame was initially far from eternal, and it was frequently extinguished by floods and storms. A local man contacted Schimmelmann and shared that, as a boy, he enlarged the cavity where the flame rests to better protect it from the elements. Another theory reported by *The Buffalo News* in 1974 suggested that a lightning strike may have caused a brush fire that started it all. Either way, this spectacle of fire and water continues to burn on in the region's collective imagination.

Address 6121 Chestnut Ridge Road, Orchard Park, NY 14127, +1 (716) 858-8355, www3.erie.gov/parks/chestnut-ridge | Getting there By car, take US 219 S to Armor Duells Road to NY-277 S/Chestnut Ridge Road | Hours Unrestricted | Tip Discover more extraordinary natural beauty in the Southtowns by hiking along the soaring cliffs of Zoar Valley's Valentine Flats Trail (Valentine Flats Road, www.dec.ny.gov/lands/83160.html).

34 — Explore & More

Playing in Buffalo's miniature Erie Canal

At downtown's Explore and More – The Ralph C. Wilson Jr. Children's Museum – girls and boys can play with perhaps the only miniature canal in the world that sits next to its life-sized counterpart.

The "Moving Water" exhibit inside the museum recreates the city's rich waterfront history for kids. A 50-foot waterfall cascading from the second floor flows into the museum's canal, which is considerably shorter than the 363-mile waterway that connected Albany and Buffalo two centuries ago. Two tubs symbolizing Lake Erie and the Hudson River flank either side of the display. Children can take a small, plastic boat floating in "Lake Erie," fill it with Fisher-Price's Little People toys, and set the vessel in motion down the canal and through a series of locks until it reaches the "Hudson."

Nearby, a replica canal packet boat features a reading area filled with children's history books and canal-era apparel to try on. Young visitors can even experiment with a pulley and crane that would have loaded cargo onto boats. "Moving Water" is the centerpiece of the museum, which features a series of exhibits spread across multiple floors that share Buffalo's story.

The exhibit's proximity to the Erie Canal replica flowing outside the museum's windows is by design. The canal's original western terminus ran along this property long before the museum's young visitors – or their parents or grandparents – were born. The original canal fell into disuse, and the city buried it nearly a century ago, building the Buffalo Memorial Auditorium, former home of the Buffalo Sabres, in its place. After demolishing "The Aud" in 2009, Buffalo decided to reclaim this history and install replica canals on the site. "Moving Water" pays tribute to this legacy and inspires the next generation of Buffalonians to learn more about this once nearly forgotten chapter of waterfront history.

Address 130 Main Street, Buffalo, NY 14202, +1 (716) 655-5131, www.exploreandmore.org, info@exploreandmore.org | Getting there Metro Rail to Erie Canal Harbor, walk one block west; bus 8, 24 to Marine Drive & Commercial Street | Hours Wed–Fri 10am–4pm, Sat 10am–5pm, Sun 10:30am–3:30pm | Tip Bring the kids on a summer day to Wilkeson Pointe, a 15-acre park that features whimsical wind sculptures, a sandy beach, and a playground along the lakeshore (225 Fuhrmann Boulevard, www.buffalowaterfront.com/venue/wilkeson-pointe).

35 — F. Scott Fitzgerald Home

A literary giant's early creative education

In the heart of Allentown, a charming, 19th-century dwelling holds a secret claim to fame as the boyhood home of literary giant F. Scott Fitzgerald. The prolific author of *The Great Gatsby* and other American classics spent two of his formative childhood years at 29 Irving Place, a house that his biographer Andrew Turnbull described as "a lovely spot for a poet to grow up in," as *The Buffalo News* recalled in a 1994 article.

Nothing at this private address draws attention to its famous past resident. Yet of the four places in Buffalo that Fitzgerald lived in as a boy from 1898 to 1908, three of which remain standing, it was this house and the surrounding Allentown neighborhood that seemingly left the deepest impression on him. Irving Place itself, which the *News* described in 1964 as a "club that looks like a street," proved to be the perfect childhood playground for the future author, with its tree-lined homes and Japanese lanterns that residents at the time hung from front porches on summer nights.

Fitzgerald's father Edward first brought the family to Buffalo from Minnesota for a job opportunity when the author was just a toddler. Save for a short stint in Syracuse, NY, the Fitzgeralds remained here until a decade later, when Edward's job loss at Procter & Gamble prompted the Fitzgeralds to move back to the Midwest.

But living on Irving Place provided Fitzgerald with proximity to downtown's many theaters, which helped foster the boy's creative spirit. Fitzgerald began taking dance lessons around this time and watched shows with his friend Hamilton Wende at the Teck Theater on Main Street. The pair would then re-enact plays in a neighbor's attic and charge for admission, the *News* later noted. Wandering Allentown's many art galleries and performance venues today, it isn't hard to imagine how this Bohemian neighborhood gave rise to an American literary icon.

Address 29 Irving Place, Buffalo, NY 14201 | Getting there Bus 11, 25 to Delaware Avenue & Allen Street | Hours Unrestricted from the outside only | Tip Walk around the corner to see the Lenox Hotel, where the Fitzgeralds lived in an apartment for a time before moving to Irving Place (140 North Street, www.lenoxhotelandsuites.com).

36 The Fenian Memorial
That time the Irish invaded Canada

Buffalo shares several miles of the longest peaceful international border in the world, but the swiftly flowing Niagara River dividing the city from Canada wasn't always so friendly. Along the river, a small memorial at the foot of Hertel Avenue marks where hundreds of Irish American Civil War veterans launched an ill-fated invasion of Canada in 1866.

The black stone monument is the only sign that this serene riverside park filled with benches and green space was the launching point for an international incident. The Fenian Invasion was "a curious episode – one of the most singular in the long history of a frontier by no means devoid of singular episodes," Frank H. Severance, the secretary of the Buffalo Historical Society, wrote back in 1921. The Fenians, a group of Irish Americans resolved to free Ireland from British rule, had planned to gather in several spots near the Canadian border in the spring of 1866. They reasoned that invading and gaining control of Canada, then under British rule, would provide them with the leverage needed to gain independence in the Emerald Isle.

Only the Buffalo contingent of several hundred soldiers ultimately set out on the night of May 31, 1866 from the docks of the Pratt Iron Works, now Tow Path Park. The group, led by Major General John O'Neill, crossed the Niagara under the cover of darkness and scored a victory against British soldiers the following day at the Battle of Ridgeway. Their momentum, however, was short lived. Reinforcements of British troops and pressure from the US Government forced the brigade to retreat back to Buffalo, where they were detained and ultimately released. The memorial credits the incident with building momentum for Ireland's eventual independence in 1922. Perhaps this long-forgotten invasion launched from Buffalo's shores really did alter the course of Irish history.

Address Tow Path Park, Foot of Hertel Avenue, Buffalo, NY 14207, www3.erie.gov/parks/tow-path | Getting there Bus 5, 23, 32, 40, 77 to Hertel Avenue & Niagara Street | Hours Unrestricted | Tip The Irish Famine Memorial pays tribute to those who lost their lives in The Great Famine, and it rests near the place where Irish immigrants first arrived on Buffalo's waterfront (40 La Riviere Drive, www.irishfaminememorials.com/2014/01/16/buffalo-new-york-1997).

37 The Flight of Five Locks

Experience an engineering marvel for yourself

The United States might look very different today if it weren't for the completion of five narrow locks along the Erie Canal in Niagara County two centuries ago.

The Flight of Five Locks, which once were lauded as one of the world's greatest engineering marvels, changed the course of American history. These remnants of the iconic waterway's early years sit tucked away in the heart of Lockport next to the present-day canal system. Visitors can walk down a trail leading from Canal Street to see the staircase locks, the surrounding stone walls, and the enormous and recently restored wooden gate doors separating each 12-foot-deep compartment. During warmer months, water cascades through the locks, which serve as a spillway for the nearby modern canal. Guided tours on summer days give guests the chance to open and close a lock door, and a small museum near the bottom of the locks brings Lockport's canal heyday to life.

No other stretch of the 363-mile canal proved as difficult to construct as the route through central Niagara County. Canal builders had to navigate the Niagara Escarpment, a 450-million-year-old rock formation extending from Western New York through Canada, which presented an extraordinary challenge to ascend. They chose the site of present-day Lockport because the escarpment's elevation there was only 60 feet.

A teacher by trade, Nathan Roberts submitted the winning design for the Flight of Five. Then an army of 2,000 laborers brought Roberts' vision to life, often risking their own lives in treacherous conditions. The canal's completion – and the nation's commerce – hinged on the Flight of Five's success. "It really epitomized the challenge of man versus nature," said Dave Kinyon, chairman of the Lockport Locks Heritage District. "The ability to overcome some of those natural obstacles is best reflected in the challenge of the Flight of Five."

Address 80 Canal Street, Lockport, NY 14094, +1 (716) 349-7998, www.locksdistrict.com, info@locksdistrict.com | Getting there Bus 44 to Main & Pine Streets, walk north on Pine Street, turn left on Ontario Street, then left on Canal Street | Hours Unrestricted | Tip Learn more about Lockport's rich canal history at the Erie Canal Discovery Center, which features a series of interactive exhibits (24 Church Street, Lockport, www.niagarahistory.org/ECDC.html).

38 _ Founding Fathers Pub
Have a beer with Buffalo's quizmaster

There are too many pieces of presidential memorabilia to count inside Founding Fathers Pub, according to owner and trivia master Michael Driscoll, who is glad he doesn't "have to dust them all." This nearly 40-year-old tavern inside a former livery stable dating back to 1874 is as much a presidential museum as it is a watering hole. Commander-in-chief portraits, campaign posters, pins, and other keepsakes line nearly every square inch of the tavern.

You'll see newspaper clippings from election nights, a Betsy Ross-shaped bourbon bottle and a can of Billy Carter's beer on a shelf, stained-glass windows filled with presidential pictures, and even a painting of General Washington crossing the Delaware on one of the pub's giant hamburgers. Dozens of flags from around the world donated by customers hang from the ceiling of this brick-walled tavern, which also boasts a complimentary popcorn machine.

Driscoll started amassing memorabilia decades ago, while he was teaching high school social studies and waiting for a permanent position to open up in suburban Buffalo. When that didn't pan out, he took the memorabilia he planned to fill his classroom with and opened a bar instead. He carries his love of teaching and history into his bartending on Friday and Saturday nights by peppering patrons with a variety of trivia questions. What's the only US state that ends with the letter K? (New York) What year was the Erie Canal completed in Buffalo? (1825) And on the first Tuesday of every month, Founding Fathers fills to the brim with trivia night contestants eager to answer questions correctly from Buffalo's unofficial quizmaster. After nearly 40 years of bartending, it has never grown old for Driscoll, one of the legends of Buffalo's bar scene.

"People always ask me, 'When are you going to retire?'" Driscoll said. "I retired when I bought this building."

Address 75 Edward Street, Buffalo, NY 14202, +1 (716) 855-8944 | **Getting there** Bus 11, 25 to Delaware Avenue & Edward Street | **Hours** Wed & Thu 3:30pm – midnight, Fri & Sat 11:30 – 3am, Sun 5pm – midnight | **Tip** During the winter months, The Place, another classic tavern, makes one of the city's top seasonal cocktails, the Tom and Jerry, and serves it in a commemorative, take-home mug (229 Lexington Avenue, www.theplacebuffalo.com).

39__ The Foundry

A bustling maker space for all

"The Foundry is a place of possibility," executive director Megan McNally said. "It's whatever you make of it, whatever you need it to be."

If the Foundry isn't all things to all people, it certainly aspires to be. This century-old former commercial laundry on a tucked-away East-Side street features dozens of maker spaces, workshops, classrooms, and digital laboratories for the community to use. On any given day, a Swedish spoon carving class might take place around the corner from a company making bottle openers out of hockey pucks and a candlemaker using a 3D printer to perfect his designs. Down the hallway, the smell of sawdust and grind of table saws greet guests as they enter the wood shop, while high school students in the nearby metal shop weld together colorful garden stakes. More than two dozen small businesses base themselves within The Foundry's low-rent incubator spaces to make products like bird feeders, T-shirts, and clocks. And at-risk students and a variety of community members use the facility to gain new skills. After taking a safety training class, guests can pay what they wish to utilize The Foundry's equipment and shops.

The organization began a decade ago, when a handful of makers and creatives banded together to create an incubator space filled with tools for the community to use. A successful Kickstarter crowd-funding campaign inspired the group to make its new home in a neighborhood that historically lacked access to such resources.

The items made by the Foundry's students and community members dot neighborhoods across Buffalo, from dozens of "take a book, leave a book" little wooden libraries lining its streets to trellises and benches found in community gardens throughout the city. Visit during open maker hours to see the space abuzz with activity and filled with community members changing the course of Buffalo with every item they make.

Address 298 Northampton Street, Buffalo, NY 14208, +1 (716) 885-1381, www.thefoundrybuffalo.org, info@thefoundrybuffalo.org | Getting there Bus 18 to Jefferson Avenue & Northampton Street, walk west | Hours See website for open maker space hours; Tours Sat 11am | Tip Borrow from a collection of thousands of tools for your next do-it-yourself project at The Tool Library, which lends them out for a nominal annual membership fee (5 W Northrup Place, www.thetoollibrary.org).

40 The Freedom Wall

Telling the stories of Civil Rights trailblazers

Large, colorful portraits of 28 Black leaders gaze out at passing motorists along Michigan Avenue and East Ferry Street. Each panel of *The Freedom Wall* (2017) honors Civil Rights trailblazers and community activists from both the past and present and from Buffalo and beyond.

"Mama" Charlene Caver Miller, a prolific volunteer who opens her East Side home to those in need, is near famed Montgomery civil rights activist Rosa Parks. Dr. Lydia T. Wright, Buffalo's first African American pediatrician and a Board of Education member, is next to renowned social reformer Frederick Douglass. And Dr. Martin Luther King, Jr. is side-by-side with Frank Merriweather, the founder of the century-old *Buffalo Criterion*, the city's oldest Black-owned weekly newspaper.

The Freedom Wall is one of the most celebrated works from the Buffalo AKG ART Museum's Public Art Initiative, which transforms blank walls and façades across the city into colorful, inspiring art spaces. The noise reduction wall at the back of the bus garage located along the Michigan Street African American Heritage Corridor proved to be the perfect canvas for this project, according to Public Art Curator Aaron Ott. The AKG Museum organized a steering committee from Buffalo's Black community that narrowed down a list of hundreds of names to the final 28 subjects, each of whom demonstrates that the fight for racial equality requires both local and national leadership.

For Edreys Wajed, one of the project's four muralist artists, *The Freedom Wall* represents a premier cultural institution successfully engaging with Buffalo's Black community. "It could be seen as the time when an institution abides by and shows empathy for a community that's been trampled over for years and decades," Wajed said. "*The Freedom Wall* was one of those linchpins for conversations to start bending in the right direction."

Address Michigan Avenue & East Ferry Street, Buffalo, NY 14209, www.albrightknox.org/community/ak-public-art/freedom-wall | Getting there Bus 13 to Michigan Avenue & East Ferry Street | Hours Unrestricted | Tip Look for *Love Black*, a mural also by Edreys Wajed, located downtown (712 Main Street, www.albrightknox.org/community/ak-public-art/love-black).

41 Gadawski's

A Polish tavern filled with Fighting Irish flair

No trip to Niagara Falls is complete without a visit to Gadawski's, the century-old Polish restaurant and bar brimming with Fighting Irish spirit. Notre Dame University paraphernalia covers nearly every square inch of this neighborhood tavern, from the championship banners lining the ceiling panels to the Fighting Irish wallpaper and themed license plates, hand towels, clocks, and vintage football team photos hanging from the walls. A Polish menu of $1.50 pierogi, cabbage roll specials on Thursdays, and a bottle of Krupnik behind the bar complement the Notre Dame décor.

The late, longtime owner of the bar Eddie Gadawski was one of the football team's greatest fans. According to Eddie's son Fred, Gadawski first started rooting for the Fighting Irish when he was a child, listening to games on the radio, because his father had told him, "Follow these guys. They're Catholics." Eddie never attended Notre Dame, but started traveling to games after he left the service in the 1950s – and never stopped. The university's alumni association even donated a vintage stadium bench to the pub following Eddie's death at 97 in 2017.

While Eddie tended bar, it was his late wife Irene who developed the Polish recipes that still fill the menu to this day. Irene lived almost her entire life over the tavern, growing up there after her father, Anthony Jankowski, first opened it in the 1920s. Large portraits of Eddie and Irene overlook the restaurant that their three children continue to run today.

Gadawski's is one of the last businesses standing on this otherwise desolate stretch of a once-proud Polish business district not far from downtown. But the steady stream of locals who enjoy $3 bottled beers and hearty, homemade Polish fare at Western New York's unofficial Fighting Irish headquarters will ensure this Niagara Falls institution remains for many more years to come.

Address 1445 Falls Street, Niagara Falls, NY 14303, +1 (716) 282-7246, www.facebook.com/gadawskis | Getting there Bus 50 to Niagara Street & Portage Road | Hours Wed 11am–2pm, Thu 11am–4pm, Fri 11am–8:30pm | Tip Niagara Falls' Polish Nook restaurant has been serving traditional Polish fare since 1964 (2242 Cudaback Avenue, www.polishnook.com).

42_Gay Bingo
"You don't have to be gay to play!"

At the beginning of every Buffalo Gay Bingo event, drag queen and mistress of ceremonies Patsy DeCline takes to the stage and leads the audience in the Bingo Pledge. "I solemnly swear that I am here to help people living with HIV and AIDS. And to stop this horrible epidemic. I also swear that bingo is just a STUUUUUUUUPID, little game! But I will keep playing Gay Bingo until this crisis is over!"

Welcome to what founder Michael Warner describes as "Not your grandmother's bingo." This loud, rollicking evening filled with raunchy jokes, double entendres, and colorful language attracts a crowd of hundreds to the bingo hall inside the Amvets Medallion Post #13 in Riverside, bucking the decades-long decline in the game's popularity. As numbers are called, the crowd of all ages chimes in with rehearsed reactions finely tuned over years of Gay Bingo. "B-1" prompts the hall to sing "One! Singular sensation, every little step he takes," from *A Chorus Line*. "O-69" causes the audience to cheer and do the wave. And the winner of the special bingo game "Tic-Tac-Toe" must shout out to the rest of the audience, "Tic-Tac-Toe, I'm a ho!" Buffalo Gay Bingo is a dry event, but patrons wander over to the Amvets bar next door before and afterward for cheap well drinks.

This monthly fundraiser for the AIDS Plus Fund of Western New York is one of the few gay bingo events in the country. Warner, who has lived with AIDS for years, found his inspiration for this endeavor nearly two decades ago while watching a PBS documentary about a similar event in Philadelphia, and he flew there to check it out. The rise in Buffalo Gay Bingo's popularity – and its move to the city's largest and last Amvets hall – speaks to growing acceptance of the LGBTQIA+ community here, he said. "Who ever thought we'd be doing Gay Bingo in an Amvets post?" Warner asked. "Ten years ago, this wouldn't have happened."

Address 25 Review Place, Buffalo, NY 14207, +1 (716) 854-0559, www.facebook.com/
BuffGayBingo, buffalogaybingo@gmail.com | **Getting there** Bus 5 to Tonawanda & Ontario
Streets, or 23, 26 to Ontario Street & Riverside High School | **Hours** Sep–Jun, second
Sat 7–10pm | Tip Continue supporting Buffalo's AIDS Community by shopping at the
Serendipity Thrift Shoppe inside First Presbyterian Church (One Symphony Circle,
www.buffaloserendipityshoppe.com).

43 Gentner Commission Market

Be part of a Springville tradition

Every Wednesday morning at Gentner Commission Market in Springville starts very much as it has for the last 80 years. Shortly after dawn, farmers from across Western New York converge on this rural auction house with sheep, cows, pigs, chickens, and goats in tow to prepare for the big day ahead. By mid morning, a flea market with dozens of vendors is under way, featuring table after table in front and behind the auction house, filled with everything from fresh, squeaky cheese curds to dolls, tools, household items, and antiques.

In the afternoon, third-generation owner Damon Gentner assumes his position at a podium in the auction house, putting to work the rapid-fire auctioneering skills he learned at the Missouri Auction School, as bushels of corn, boxes of eggs, live cows, and goats all go up for bid.

"Would you bid 30? I've got 30. Would you give 40? 40? I've got 40. Would you hit 50?" he says in quick succession to the auction room, a large space filled with wooden stadium seating for 200. Gentner has kept the Wednesday auction tradition alive from his late father Billy and his grandfather Raymond before him, who started the auction in 1939 as a way to procure more cattle for his farm. The auction continues to serve as an economic lifeline for farmers across the region and as a place for all Western New Yorkers to find a bargain or some entertainment on a Wednesday.

Gentner, the youngest of nine children, has seen everything under the sun arrive at his flea market and auction – even an inscribed tombstone from a couple undergoing a divorce who decided they didn't want to keep each other company in the afterlife. "From the time the sun comes up, it is just crankin'," Gentner said. "It's honkin' and jukin'. You never know what you'll see here."

Address 341 W Main Street, Springville, NY 14141, +1 (716) 592-4062, www.facebook.com/ gentnerscommissionmarket, gentnercm@gmail.com | Getting there By car, take US-219 S to NY-39 E | Hours Mon&Tue 8am–8pm, Wed 8am–9pm | Tip Wendel's Poultry Farm sponsors a chicken barbecue every weekend from May to October and sells chicken pot pies and other fresh poultry products from its store (12466 Vaughn Street, East Concord, www.wendelspoultryfarm.com).

44 George & Company
New tricks at an old magic shop

One of Buffalo's oldest stores has stood the test of time by selling whoopie cushions, stink bombs, jumping beans, and thousands of other novelty items, magic tricks, and costumes.

George & Company features shelves lined with floating plastic eyeballs to place in beverages, buzzers that send electric shocks via a handshake, phony parking tickets, exploding pens, itching powder, and a wide variety of fake feces. This is Buffalo's one-stop shop for the "horribly hilarious" nail through the head gag, magic mirrors, invisible dog leashes, vanishing beer cans, hot pepper candy (ages 14+), and mouth coils that "produce yards and yards of streamers from your mouth!"

Behind the store counter, manager Karen Noe knows literally every trick in the book from 40 years of experience. Noe can teach customers almost any magic trick and illusion you can think of, from the "baffling bag" that changes colors every time it turns inside out, to the "magic sponge ball," three-card monte, and dice tricks. The shop, which created the popular dice game "Left Right Center," also features one of Buffalo's best selections of puzzles, board games, Halloween costumes, chess sets, and brain teasers.

George has owned George & Company since back in 1916, when George Smilanich Sr. purchased the Buffalo Novelty Bazaar on Swan Street and soon renamed the store. It was his son, George Smilanich, Jr., who broadened its offerings to include more magic tricks, games, and novelty items to meet the rising demand from Baby Boomer children. Today, George III owns the store, and George IV and George V might just follow in his footsteps. The store was a fixture for years downtown before moving to Williamsville in the 1990s. "Buffalo's Most Unusual Store" sells the gift of human connection through humor and wonder, an increasingly rare experience in the age of the smartphone.

Address 4261 Transit Road, Williamsville, NY 14221, +1 (716) 633-0711, www.georgeandcompany.co, georgeandco6850@gmail.com | **Getting there** By car, take NY-5 E and turn south on Transit Road | **Hours** Mon–Sat 10am–6pm, Sun 11am–4pm | **Tip** The BFLO store, located in the same shopping plaza, offers one of the region's largest selections of Buffalo-themed merchandise (4199 Transit Road, Williamsville, www.bfloshop.com).

45 Gondola Macaroni Company

Taste Buffalo's rich pasta-making legacy

There's no other pasta in the world that tastes quite like the ravioli, stuffed shells, and noodles sold at Gondola Macaroni Company – and that's by design. Founder Guido Colla built each pasta machine himself when he first opened Gondola in Buffalo's Black Rock neighborhood more than 50 years ago. Colla grew up in Passagno, Italy, in a family that owned a deli. He first emigrated to Buffalo to take a job as a machinist at Buffalo's legendary Gioia Macaroni Plant. As the family story goes, Colla combined his passion for pasta and his expertise as a machinist to custom build his own equipment after a $1,000 settlement from a car accident allowed him to strike out on his own. He and his wife Maria opened Gondola, their very own pasta company.

The Collas made pasta from their Potomac Avenue home for a decade before opening the production facility and retail store at Niagara and Austin Streets in 1968 that's now run by their granddaughter Wendy Colla-Bianco. Gondola's staff still makes the pasta in a small room facing Niagara Street much as it always has. Employees begin mixing the ravioli fillings by 7:30am, preparing the dough by 8am, and continue working on the pasta all day until 5pm. Wendy's mother Sharon even still hand-stuffs each shell with cheese as she has for years.

Gondola cuts no corners, using real potatoes for its gnocchi and top round for the filling in its beef ravioli – just as Guido and Maria Colla did. Coolers filled with freshly made pasta and sauce line the retail store up front. Even as some of Guido's original machines head into retirement, his granddaughter replicates new machines to a tee, ensuring Gondola's unique taste remains intact. "I love the fact that hopefully I'm living out my grandfather's American dream," Wendy said. "I don't know if he ever thought it would be going on this long."

Address 1985 Niagara Street, Buffalo, NY 14207, +1 (716) 874-4280, www.gondolamacaroni.com | Getting there Bus 5, 32 to Niagara & Austin Streets | Hours Mon – Sat 9:30am – 4:30pm | Tip Down the street is Santasiero's Restaurant, a 100-year-old tavern painted in the colors of the Italian flag that serves steaming bowls of *pasta e fagioli* and homemade sauce (1329 Niagara Street, www.facebook.com/santasieros).

46 Hamburg Brewing Company

Come for the beer, stay for the secret model trains

One of the largest model train sets in the Eastern United States sits hidden behind the beer production vats of Hamburg Brewing Company. The 2,500-square-foot train set took two years to build by hand and features a replica of the San Jacinto Mountain range near Durango, Colorado. The model boasts several miniature towns, more than 10,000 model trees, three waterfalls, and 800 feet of functioning track capable of running nine trains simultaneously. Little hidden Easter eggs abound in the set, from the Mount Rushmore re-creation with the heads of the Three Stooges to a "red light" district in one of the villages, where all the exterior lamps burn red.

The train set was the brainchild of brothers John and Joe Russo, who had been collecting trains since they were children and decided in the late 1990s to create a train museum inside a building they originally constructed to house their muscle car collection. There are nods to the Russo family throughout the set, such as Anna Mae's General Store, named after their mother, and an homage to Buffalo's former Sorrento cheese plant, which their father Joe founded in 1947.

The brothers completed about 80 percent of the museum but never opened it. Instead, they pivoted to beer a decade ago when they opened Hamburg Brewing Company, which offers signature brews, like Lakeside Lager, in its lodge-like taproom and expansive beer garden.

The giant train set, which was the second largest in the US upon its completion in 2001, will likely remain tucked behind the production room, and you can see it by setting up a tour in advance. "It was so big and so customized and so intricate that you could not tear it down and move it. It will remain here forever," said John Russo, who worked on the set with his father John and uncle Joe. "You cannot duplicate it."

Address 6553 Boston State Road, Hamburg, NY 14075, +1 (716) 649-3249, www.hamburgbrewing.com | Getting there By car, take US 219 S to NY-391 W | Hours Brewery: Tue 4–10pm, Wed–Sat noon–10pm, Sun 10am–8pm; train tours by appointment | Tip Sample only-in-Buffalo beers like Sponge Candy Stout and Loganberry Wit inside Resurgence Brewing Company along Buffalo's waterfront (55 Chicago Street, www.resurgencebrewing.com).

47 The Hermit's Cascade

Former stomping grounds of a legendary recluse

Tucked upriver behind Niagara Falls is a much smaller cascade dedicated to a famous recluse who roamed here two centuries ago. When you're crossing the bridge connecting Goat and Three Sisters Islands in Niagara Falls State Park, you might not even notice the Hermit's Cascade flowing underneath you. The small, unmarked waterfall was a favorite hangout for Francis Abbott, known as the Hermit of Niagara, who arrived here in 1829 with a roll of blankets, a flute, a walking stick, and a sense of adventure.

Abbott was a well-read polyglot and world traveler who spoke with a British accent, preferred a steady diet of wheat flour mixed into water, and had friends back in England supporting his adventures. Entranced by the "sublime spectacle" of the falls, Abbott ultimately decided to never leave. He found a spare room in the only house standing on Goat Island and then constructed his own cabin near present-day Prospect Point.

"Can it be that there are those who come to this place, and leave it in one day! I am astonished that persons can be found so little interested in these astonishing works of nature," Abbott told Judge Samuel DuVeaux, who relayed Abbott's story in the 1839 book, *The Falls of Niagara*.

The Hermit of Niagara became a larger-than-life figure. Visitors often noticed him walking up and down the river playing a guitar minstrel-style and holding a sign that requested he be left alone. He was a fixture along the 300-foot Terrapin Bridge that led to the edge of the falls, where he would hang by his hands over the brink. But his stay was ultimately short-lived. Nearly two years after he arrived, Abbott drowned near the base of the falls while bathing. Little remains today to remind visitors of this legendary character. So, on your next visit, make sure to discover this small cascade and pay tribute to one of the most eccentric personalities to ever call the falls home.

Address 332 Prospect Street, Niagara Falls, NY 14303, +1 (716) 278-1794, www.niagarafallsstatepark.com | **Getting there** By car, drive to Goat Island, and proceed to the parking lot next to Three Sisters Islands to find the path that leads to the cascade | **Hours** Daily dawn–dusk | **Tip** Continue walking past the cascade to the end of Three Sisters Islands for one of the best views of the Niagara River rapids upstream from the falls (Niagara Falls State Park, Niagara Falls, www.niagarafallsstatepark.com).

48 Herschell Carrousel Factory Museum

What goes around comes around

North Tonawanda hosts the only museum where visitors can explore the history of merry-go-rounds inside a former factory that made them. For nearly 100 years, the city that bills itself as the "Home of the Carousel" and hangs carved horses from its street posts produced one of America's favorite amusement park rides. The Herschell Carrousel Factory Museum guides you through recreated assembly lines, where employees of the Alan Herschell Company built the iconic rides generations ago.

You can explore the step-by-step process on the museum's carving floor, from the pile of lumber to the sanded wooden horse heads and hooves on work tables, and carving tools donated by former employees. You'll see more than 50 wooden horses, and your visit concludes with a ride on a restored 1916 carousel inside the roundhouse, where the company once tested its products. "All museums are interesting. But not all museums are fun," Director Ian Seppala says. "At this museum, you can learn about the past while having a good time, too."

Allan Herschell decided to add carousel-making to his existing farm equipment factory in North Tonawanda in 1872 after seeing one during a trip to New York City. At one time, his company and its successors made up to half of all wooden carousels in operation throughout the US, a surge in demand that coincided with the halcyon days of the American amusement park. After the company folded in 1970, concerned community members, elected officials, and former employees saved the deteriorating plant and preserved it as a museum, which opened in 1984. The museum embodies the collective will of a community determined to preserve its legacy and proves that what goes around really does come around.

Address 180 Thompson Street, North Tonawanda, NY 14120, +1 (716) 693-1885, www.carrouselmuseum.org, info@carrouselmuseum.org | Getting there Bus 25 to Oliver & Thompson Streets | Hours See website for seasonal hours | Tip Take a ride on the Buffalo Heritage Carousel, a restored, solar-powered 1920s merry-go-round made and lovingly restored in North Tonawanda (44 Prime Street, www.buffaloheritagecarousel.org).

49 _ Hibbard's Original Custard
Rich frozen treats for generations

No roadside stand in Western New York arguably sells frozen custard as rich and creamy as Hibbard's Original Custard, a mainstay in Lewiston since 1939. Staff arrive to make the custard from scratch hours before the stand with the white-and-blue awning opens for the day. They choose seven flavors to feature daily from a repertoire of several dozen options, like cinnamon toast crunch, piña colada, and strawberry cheesecake, while chocolate, vanilla, black raspberry, and pistachio are always on the menu. There's even the "Big Barenaked Bang," a coffee flavor inspired by the Barenaked Ladies, who frequent the stand when they perform at nearby Artpark.

Hibbard's uses less air in its production than other custard stands in Buffalo, creating a product so dense that it needs to be scooped out of a cooler like hard-serve. But the comparisons between this custard, which mixes in eggs to create a creamier, richer product, and ice cream end there. "If you have had ice cream before, our custard blows it out of the water," said co-owner Kristen Trunzo.

Hibbard's has certainly expanded its flavor list since Trunzo's grandfather Harold Hibbard first began selling frozen custard with his proprietary vanilla flavor still used to this day. He first learned of the frozen treat while wintering in St. Petersburg, Florida, where a neighbor who had recently opened a custard stand in Wisconsin – long considered America's custard capital – inspired him to do the same. Hibbard realized that Western New York's abundance of dairy farms could supply this new frozen novelty and shipped in custard mix by rail on an insulated boxcar to begin selling his product.

With his six grandchildren still at the helm ensuring quality and consistency and serving custard from the same machines for generations, it's no wonder Hibbard's has endured as a beloved mainstay for nearly a century.

Address 105 Portage Road, Lewiston, NY 14092, +1 (716) 754-4218, www.hibbardscustard.com | Getting there By car, take Niagara Scenic Parkway N to NY-18F N | Hours See website for seasonal hours | Tip East Hill Creamery has one of the only vending machines in North America that sells cheese (346 S Main Street, Perry, www.easthillcreamery.com).

50 Hispanic Heritage District
Taste this neighborhood's rich heritage

Along a stretch of Niagara Street known as Avenida San Juan, visitors can taste the flavors and explore the rich history of the city's Latin American community. The restaurants, public art, street banners, and historical signage found along this Lower West Side thoroughfare reflect the neighborhood's rich Hispanic heritage.

Inside Sabores De Mi Tierra, the city's sole Colombian restaurant, salsa and merengue music plays as staff sell pieces of pork belly a la carte and prepare *bandeja paisa* breakfasts of sausage, beans, and rice behind the counter. A few blocks up the street, the aroma of chicken and beef *pastelillos* fresh out of the fryer fills the air at La Flor Bakery, which stocks its shelves with Puerto Rican pastries, like the *quesito* (cheese) turnover and the *tres leches* cake. And across the street at the Niagara Cafe, customers buy plates of rotisserie chicken with sides of plantain chips and wash them down with cans of Tropic-cola.

Generations of Latin Americans moved to the area, found jobs as factory workers and farm hands, and ultimately settled in this neighborhood close to downtown. But it was only a decade ago when the Hispanic Heritage Council worked to brand this area as the Hispanic Heritage District to serve as a catalyst for its revitalization. "We want to be a showplace for our visitors," said Casimiro Rodriguez, the council's past president. "The community deserves it. It's long overdue."

The council secured funding to add banners to the street poles, highlighting important neighborhood residents and historical signage that resembles Puerto Rican fortresses along the sidewalks. Soon after, murals illustrating Latin homelands, the migration to North America, and Roberto Clemente began to dot the streetscape, and new investment followed. This neighborhood has begun to chart a new course for its future by fully embracing its proud past.

Address Niagara Street between Porter Avenue & Georgia Street, Buffalo, NY 14201, +1 (716) 402-1442, www.hispanicheritagewny.org/heritage-district.php, info@hispanicheritagewny.org | Getting there Bus 5 to Niagara & Jersey Streets | Hours Unrestricted | Tip Continue your Latin American food tour at La Divina Tacos, which features authentic Mexican street food (2896 Delaware Avenue, Kenmore, www.facebook.com/LaDivinaUno).

51 Hoyt Lake

Ride on a FLOATmingo or a Buffalo-made rowboat

Hoyt Lake in Delaware Park features two of Buffalo's most unique watercraft rentals: the pink FLOATmingos and a fleet of wooden rowboats handcrafted by local high-school students.

Rental operator Paul Koessler has heard people call the bird-themed boats floating in Hoyt Lake those "pink chickens" and "pink swan-looking things." The Buffalo Maritime Center's rentable avian flotilla actually depicts flamingos, the tropical bird previously known here as a kitschy lawn ornament. Each one of the 10 FLOATmingo pedal boats available for rent next to the Marcy Casino has a Buffalo-themed name, from "Bird on Weck" and "Billa Flotilla," to "Cheeri-FLO" and "Floganberry." Visitors can choose a two- or four-person FLOAT-mingo and pedal the length of Hoyt Lake, a 30-minute journey past lush greenery and a gushing fountain. Koessler ordered the boats after seeing the inflatable pink FLOmingo, which the Buffalo Olmsted Parks Conservancy placed in the lake to celebrate landscape architect Frederick Law Olmsted's 150th birthday.

The FLOATmingos may be attention-grabbing, but the rowboats arguably offer a more uniquely Buffalo experience. A group of high-school students spend an entire academic year constructing several rowboats by hand inside the Arthur Street warehouse of the Buffalo Maritime Center, which specializes in wooden boatbuilding. Twice each week for 90 minutes per day, the students sand, buff, and trans-form white oak and cypress into a fleet of sturdy vessels that last for years. Each boat takes 100 hours to produce. "There's a lot of crafts-manship and hard work that goes into building those boats, a lot of effort and mindfulness," said Chelsea Moore, the Maritime Center's education and outreach coordinator. Both the rowboats and the FLOATmingos offer an unforgettable way to explore an urban lake that most have only viewed from shore.

Address 199 Lincoln Parkway, Buffalo, NY 14222, +1 (716) 881-0111, www.buffalomaritimecenter.org, info@buffalomaritimecenter.org | Getting there Bus 20 to Rockwell Road, walk north and turn right on Iroquois Drive, then turn right on Lincoln Parkway | Hours See website for seasonal rentals | Tip Tour where the students constructed the rowboats at the Buffalo Maritime Center, which produces wooden boats of all shapes and sizes and features a small museum dedicated to the craft (90 Arthur Street, www.buffalomaritimecenter.org/visit/#arthur).

52 Humboldt-Hospital Station

Where art elevates the downtrodden

For the cost of a $2 fare, subway riders can explore one of Buffalo's greatest cultural treasures hiding in plain sight: the captivating portraits by world-renowned photographer Milton Rogovin. Rogovin's 1985 installation *Working People* features several portraits of blue-collar Buffalonians clad in steel plant uniforms stained with sweat, as they stare out at passing commuters inside Buffalo's Humboldt-Hospital subway station. One steel plant worker, carrying a chain over her shoulder, looks warily into the camera. Another worker, goggles raised and shovel in hand, appears paused in between his daily tasks.

The four-decade-old pictures, tucked far below Main Street at the bottom of two escalators, are part of a public art series found across Buffalo's subway system. They're a reminder of a bygone era of the city, when blue-collar labor still reigned supreme. And they embody the decades-long career of Rogovin, who championed the city's downtrodden, disenfranchised, and marginalized citizens.

"(My father) just had tremendous respect for the people who worked and made the city work. He had the most respect for those who did the hardest, dirtiest, most dangerous work," said his daughter Ellen Rogovin Hart. "He just had a burning need to tell the stories of Buffalo."

Born in Brooklyn in 1909, Rogovin moved to Buffalo as a young man and spent most of his 102 years here, working for decades as an optometrist. But the FBI noticed his political activities, and the *Buffalo Evening News* labeled him as "Buffalo's Top Red" in a front-page article in 1957. His career sidelined, Rogovin picked up a camera and began to help the public see the world more clearly through photography instead. Pay a visit to this quiet subway station platform to remember the man who provided a voice to Buffalo's voiceless through his extraordinary vision.

Address 2040 Main Street, Buffalo, NY 14208, www.metro.nfta.com | **Getting there** Metro Rail to Humboldt-Hospital | **Hours** Unrestricted | **Tip** See more public art inside Buffalo's subway system on an Explore Buffalo Art of the Subway tour (www.explorebuffalo.org).

53 The Iron Island Museum
Spookiest Site in the City

Strange occurrences and paranormal encounters began happening in 2000. That's when the Iron Island Preservation Society moved into its new space in Buffalo's Lovejoy neighborhood – in a former church that is also a former funeral parlor. Staff setting up the Iron Island Museum here swore they saw shadowy figures in rooms and along hallways. Picture frames flew off of tables and onto the floor. Ghost hunters picked up sounds of musket fire surrounding the military uniforms on display and of a child's voice saying the word, "boat." Lights turned on and off inside the museum when no one else was around.

Museum staff found two dozen urns of cremated human remains in the basement shortly after moving in, which curator Marge Hastreiter believes is one reason why restless spirits haunt the site. "It doesn't have to be Friday the 13th or Halloween or a full moon. It can happen day or night," Hastreiter said. "There was so much sadness in here. Maybe these people weren't loved … I think they just want to be noticed."

The Iron Island Museum, named after the neighborhood's moniker earned from the railroad tracks that surrounded the area, is as much of a haunted site as it is a tribute to the city's far East Side. You may recognize some of the neighborhood memorabilia on display, from a barber chair and a preserved church altar, to railroad workers' lanterns and black-and-white, Catholic grade-school pictures, adorning the walls and rooms. The Museum originally opened as a church in 1883 before it was converted into a funeral home in the 1950s.

You can also sit in comfy parlor chairs left over from the funeral home and wait to see if you're lucky enough to encounter a spirit at the museum, which offers guided historical tours, ghost tours and overnight investigations by request. This is a place to learn about how generations of Lovejoy residents lived – and perhaps even to meet a local resident or two from the afterlife.

Address 998 E Lovejoy Street, Buffalo, NY 14206, +1 (716) 892-3084, www.ironislandmuseum.com | Getting there Bus 1 to E Lovejoy & Green Streets | Hours See website for schedule | Tip Drive down the lakeshore to experience another haunted site, the nearly 150-year-old Dunkirk Lighthouse, which offers guided ghost hunts and paranormal investigations each fall (1 Lighthouse Point Drive, Dunkirk, www.dunkirklighthouse.com).

54__Jimmie's Shoe Repair
Meet one of Buffalo's last cobblers

Despite Joseph Bavisotto's best efforts, customers call the longtime owner of one of Buffalo's last shoe repair shops "Jimmie." Bavisotto's wife tried to clear up the confusion by gifting him a nameplate at the front of the shop with the title, *Doctor of all Shoes*, though he would have preferred "Saver of Soles." But it's an honest mistake. The sign for "Jimmie's Shoe Repair" has been displayed prominently on this Hertel Avenue storefront for generations, so most who drop off high heels, loafers, and boots address the bespectacled, septuagenarian owner and only employee by that name.

The smell of shoe polish and the din of AM talk radio greet guests as they meet Bavisotto, who stands by the wooden, 1920s cash register that maxes out at nine dollars and ninety-nine cents. Dozens of pairs of footwear awaiting pickup by their owners line shelves along the walls of the shop, which also sells bottles of shoe polish and pairs of laces. Bavisotto closely eyes every pair of shoes that customers bring to his front counter, provides an appraisal of the work needed, and gives the estimated turnaround time.

"We treat the shoes like our own. Nobody walks out of here with shoes unless I like (the job)," he said. "We do good work at a fair price." That motto has guided Bavisotto and his late father, also named Joseph, who purchased the nearly century-old Jimmie's from original owner Jimmie Martin in 1945 and moved the shop to its current address in 1959. Neither father nor son ever felt compelled to change the name of the popular shop. The younger Bavisotto, who started working there as a child and took over from his dad in 1979, estimates that he has worked on hundreds of thousands of shoes in his lifetime, from sole replacement to heel repair. Whether Jimmie or Joseph, no matter: this small storefront proves that a job well done still stands the test of time.

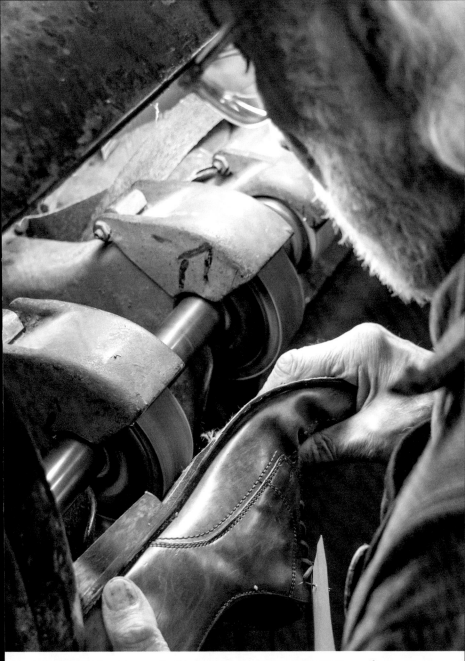

Address 1530 Hertel Avenue, Buffalo, NY 14216, +1 (716) 862-9205 | Getting there
Bus 23 to Hertel Avenue & Wellington Road | Hours Tue, Thu, Fri, & Sat 8:30am–5pm,
Wed 8:30am–1pm | Tip Continue exploring Hertel Avenue's oldest businesses
by catching a movie at the beautiful North Park Theatre, which dates back to 1920
(1428 Hertel Avenue, www.northparktheatre.org).

55 _ K Art
Indigenous art from across the continent

Indigenous artists from across the continent gather downtown to showcase their work at K Art, one of the country's only Native American-owned galleries.

This small exhibit space that opened in 2020 has featured a variety of artists working in many media, including wood carvings and bead work from Alaska; collages by a Ho-Chunk artist from Sioux City; sculptures, jewelry, and antler carvings from the Haudenosaunee; and intricate drawings on paper bags by Rochester-based artist G. Peter Jemison. K Art focuses on Indigenous artwork from the last two decades and hosts a rotating series of exhibits on its spare, white walls. A sign outside the gallery reads, *New York, Today Your Host is Seneca*, with the letters of New York spelled backwards. It welcomes guests and reminds them of the Senecas' presence throughout the region prior to European settlement.

The gallery has helped elevate the work of Native American artists by garnering international acclaim and traveling to pop-up art shows in New York City and Miami. Their talents have started conversations about what it means to be Indigenous in the 21st century, according to Gallery Associate Federico Rosario. "Now that people are becoming more aware and appreciative of Native history, we're really able to grow with it," Rosario said.

K Art is the brainchild of Dave Kimelberg, an entrepreneur and member of the Seneca Nation who spent much of his life collecting indigenous art. Kimelberg's artistic roots run deep: his mother was an art teacher, and his late brother, Michael, was an accomplished watercolor artist. Dave and Michael had talked for years about opening a gallery, which David did following his brother's death in 2018. This gallery has done more than enhance Buffalo's art scene. It has deepened an appreciation across the country for this once over-looked and immensely talented community of artists.

Address 808 Main Street, Buffalo, NY 14202, +1 (716) 216-2941, www.thek.art, contact@thek.art |
Getting there Metro Rail to Allen/Medical Campus; bus 19 to Main & Virginia Streets | Hours
Thu–Sat 11am–4pm | Tip Discover more Haudenosaunee history and culture at the Seneca
Iroquois National Museum (82 W Hetzel Street, Salamanca, www.senecamuseum.org).

56 Kleinhans Music Hall
Venue built by a love story

Buffalo owes a debt of gratitude to the husband and wife who so loved the city that they left their fortune to create a world-class concert hall still enjoyed today. Edward Kleinhans and Mary Seaton didn't live to see the completion of Kleinhans Music Hall, but they certainly would have been pleased with the end result.

The inseparable couple bonded over music. Mary was a pianist and professional singer, and Edward was the owner of a downtown men's store. They traveled to concert halls around the world during their 33-year marriage. The pair wanted Buffalo to have a venue of a similar caliber, as the city's music hall then was a former army drill shed. Soon after their deaths within three months of each other in 1934 (some say Mary died of a broken heart), Buffalo discovered that they had left $1 million to build the hall.

At the time, some people wanted a combination convention center and concert hall, but those who knew the couple's desire for an intimate venue resisted that plan. And so, the foundation that stewarded the funds brought the original dream to life in 1940 by combining the donation with New Deal federal funds. There isn't a bad seat in the house of this acoustically perfect venue designed by Eliel and Eero Saarinen. No poles or columns block the view of any patron, and no proscenium obscures the stage where the Buffalo Philharmonic Orchestra plays. Most seats on Kleinhans' lower level are at eye-level with the musicians, and the front row sits within feet of the stage.

Though the philanthropic couple never attended a concert at this National Historic Landmark, their spirit is present. "The faith of these noble benefactors … consistently spurred us on to renewed effort and high endeavor," Buffalo Foundation Vice Chairman Edwin Letchworth remarked at the hall's opening. "We stand at last, amazed, at the dazzling beauty which is the reward."

Address 3 Symphony Circle, Buffalo, NY 14201, +1 (716) 885-5000, www.kleinhansbuffalo.org |
Getting there Bus 22 to Porter & Richmond Avenues | Hours See website for upcoming events |
Tip Continue your musical tour of Symphony Circle by listening for songs played by the recently
restored carillon inside the bell tower of the First Presbyterian Church of Buffalo (1 Symphony
Circle, www.firstchurchbuffalo.org).

57___Lake Effect Ice Cream

Get the scoop on these extraordinary flavors

Lockport might have the only ice cream stand in the world that scoops out flavors infused with Loganberry, Labatt Blue, and Frank's Red Hot.

Lake Effect Ice Cream's menu doubles as a food tour through some of Western New York's favorite regional specialties. Try "Paula's Glazed Donut," made with real pieces of fry cake from the iconic local doughnut chain, or the "Revolution," with sprinkles of coffee beans roasted at Buffalo's Public Espresso. On a nostalgia kick? Sample the "Loganberry," which has the same syrupy soft drink ingredient that hooked generations of revelers at Crystal Beach Amusement Park, or the seasonal ice cream cake shaped like one of the Broadway Market's butter lambs. The "Medium Extra Creamy" is an homage to the chicken wing doused with a healthy portion of Frank's Red Hot. And "The Aud," a blend of Labatt Blue beer, peanuts, and chocolate-covered pretzels, smells just like the Buffalo Sabres' former home, the Memorial Auditorium, according to co-owner Jason Wulf.

"Once they try something new and get over the fact that it's not something they're used to, it's amazing how they keep coming back for more new things," Wulf said. "When we make something, we kind of don't hold back." Wulf and his business partner Erik Bernardi remain teachers at Lockport High School, where they sometimes bring new flavors into class for students to taste test. Many of their students spend summers working at the shop.

They first began experimenting with ice cream flavors at their homes during summer break more than 15 years ago. Each tried to one-up the other with new concoctions until the friends joined forces and started selling their ice cream at local festivals. They eventually opened two stores in Lockport and North Buffalo. In a little more than a decade, their efforts evolved from a summer lark into one of the region's must-try treats.

Address 79 Canal Street, Lockport, NY 14094, +1 (716) 201-1643, www.lakeeffecticecream.com, info@lakeeffecticecream.com | Getting there Bus 44 to Main & Pine Streets | Hours Mon – Fri 4 – 9pm, Sat & Sun noon – 9pm | Tip Enjoy another one of the region's great ice cream cones at the flagship Nick Charlap's Ice Cream, which traces its roots back to a generations-old dairy plant run by the Charlap family in the Boston Hills (7264 Boston State Road, www.nickcharlapsicecreaminc.com).

58 Lake Erie's Ice Volcanoes

Discover a frozen phenomenon

Those who venture out to the beaches along Lake Erie south of Buffalo each winter might see an extraordinary spectacle: the formation of ice volcanoes along the shoreline.

The eastern shore of Lake Erie is one of the best places in the world to view these ice formations that are unique to large bodies of freshwater. When the temperatures plunge and the winds pick up in January and February, the lake's waves form large mounds of ice as they crash onshore. The pressure from the waves carves out a hole that the warmer water rushes through and spurts out like frozen lava from the top of the mounds. Each gush of spray erupting through the ice volcanoes freezes as it escapes on exceptionally cold days, adding to their size. Along Evangola State Park's beach, dozens of ice volcanoes can form, some of which can reach a height of 15 feet – a phenomenal sight in the depths of winter.

Lake Erie, the shallowest of the Great Lakes, is especially prone to freezing in the winter and creating the conditions necessary for their formation. The prevailing westerly winds bring the waves to the lake's eastern shore, making the beaches south of Buffalo ice volcano central. Evangola, which sponsors guided ice volcano hikes each winter, is one of the best spots to look for them. Because of changing ice conditions, it's safest to view these mounds from a distance. Stay off the ice and head to the sand or the walking path above the beach's cliffs to look for them.

Ice volcanoes require at least several days of bitter cold to form, and Western New York's gradually warming winters have made it more challenging for them to take shape – and to last. Extended thaws cause them to collapse quickly. But after any long period of frigid conditions and wind, it's a safe bet that a drive to Evangola will indeed pay off with a sighting of these natural wonders of the Great Lakes.

Address 10191 Old Lake Shore Road, Irving, NY 14081, +1 (716) 549-1050, www.parks.ny.gov/parks/evangola, evangolastatepark@parks.ny.gov | Getting there By car, take Route 5 W to Evangola State Park Road, then south on Lake Road and continue on to Old Lake Shore Road | Hours Unrestricted, but call ahead to see if ice volcanoes have formed | Tip In the warmer months, explore the Evangola Nature Center to learn more about Lake Erie's fascinating ecosystem (10191 Old Lake Shore Road, Irving, www.parks.ny.gov/environment/nature-centers/16/details.aspx).

59___ The Lancaster Opera House

A legacy of excellence for over a century

One of the last venues of its kind, The Lancaster Opera House never actually hosted opera when it opened nearly 130 years ago.

Theater guests sometimes think they're in the wrong place when they arrive at this imposing brick building that towers over the village, as the only sign, above the door, reads, *TOWN HALL LANCASTER, NEW YORK.* Some will head to the first-floor assessor's office, where residents go to pay their taxes, mistakenly believing it's the box office. But you'll soon discover a 275-seat performing arts venue on the town hall's second floor that hosts a full slate of professional shows and musicals in one of the oldest theaters left in Erie County.

Back when the Lancaster Opera House first opened in the 1890s, it wasn't unusual for American town offices and theaters to be under the same roof. Lancaster's forefathers named the theater the Opera House, even though there were no scheduled operas, to conceal the fact that less wholesome events like vaudeville and burlesque sometimes took place there too, according to Opera House Executive Director David Bondrow. Eventually, most other town halls either moved into newer facilities or burned down, leaving Lancaster with one of the country's last combination buildings.

The opera house hosted commencement ceremonies, dances, recitals, and musicals until the Great Depression, when the town turned it into a food distribution center for the poor. After a stint as a Civil Defense Headquarters during the Cold War, the venue then sat vacant for decades. Residents banded together to restore it to its original luster in the 1980s – and they even began to host some evenings of opera. Today, the Opera House stands as a testament to Lancaster's determination to hold onto and build on its rich performing arts legacy.

Address 21 Central Avenue, Lancaster, NY 14086, +1 (716) 683-1776, www.lancasteropera.org |
Getting there Bus 46 to Central Avenue & Broadway | Hours Check website for showtimes; tours
by appointment | Tip Enjoy another old venue reinvigorated with new life at Lockport's Palace
Theater, which dates back to 1925 (2 East Avenue, Lockport, www.lockportpalacetheatre.org).

60   Liberty Building

Century-old advertisement above downtown Buffalo

Buffalo's skyline might just top New York City's in one regard: it has not one, but *two* Statues of Liberty gracing its skyline. The twin Statues of Liberty high atop the Liberty Building downtown are as much a reminder of a century-old corporate advertisement as they are an enduring symbol of American freedom. Architect Alfred Bossom added the statues in 1925 as the finishing touch for the new headquarters of his client, Liberty Bank. The 36-foot-tall replica statues face east and west. They blink on and off at night, thanks to 1,000-watt light bulbs that are accessible through an 18-foot-high, four-foot-wide stairwell that goes up each arm.

Liberty Bank had begun more than four decades earlier in Buffalo as the German American Bank but changed its name in 1918 as a wave of anti-German sentiment washed over the United States following World War I. When it came time to design a new headquarters, bank officials opted to place the two statues of liberty high atop their downtown Buffalo building, perhaps to prove just how patriotic they were. "They really wanted to push that brand after World War I and dispel any of the lingering German connections," Explore Buffalo Executive Director Brad Hahn said.

In an interesting twist, the step-like pedestals that support each statue, both prominent features on the building, likely reflected Bossom's recent travel experiences. The year before completing the Liberty Building, Bossom published the book, *An Architectural Pilgrimage to Mexico*, which detailed his discoveries south of the border. Each pedestal resembles an ancient Mayan or Aztec pyramid that Bossom would probably have seen while exploring. The Statues of Liberty long outlived Liberty Bank, which disappeared from Buffalo in the 1980s. But much to Buffalo's delight, the figures have remained, adding a memorable and historic touch to the city's skyline.

Address 424 Main Street, Buffalo, NY 14202, www.mainliberty.com/liberty-building | Getting there Metro Rail to Evans Bank @ Lafayette Square; bus 1, 2, 3, 4, 66, 81 to Court & Pearl Streets | Hours Unrestricted from outside only | Tip Observe the Statues of Liberty closer to eye-level from the 28th floor City Hall Observation Deck (65 Niagara Square, www.visitbuffaloniagara.com/businesses/buffalo-city-hall-observation-deck).

61 Little Summer Street

Where great gardens create great neighborhoods

"We get a lot of people who drive down the street all the time because it's pretty and because it changes," longtime Little Summer Street resident Ellie Dorritie said. "Every week it's a different show." That show starts in spring and lasts until fall, when this small, curving, one-way street in the city's Cottage District transforms into one of Buffalo's go-to garden destinations.

Hundreds of plants blossom from window boxes, flowerpots lining the sidewalk, and hanging baskets on streetlights and front porches. Flowers burst from nearly every square inch of several of the street's "hell strips" – the small patches of land between the road and the sidewalk – and its front yards. Walking down this city block, you'll find blooming sunflowers, Russian sage, gooseneck loosestrife, turtlehead, and scores of other flora that complement the brick and multi-colored cottages lining Little Summer.

When Dorritie, one of the street's leading green thumbs, first moved there in the early 1990s, the block lined with 19th-century cottages was not flowering. And Buffalonians were not clamoring to move here. Loud parties and crime in the area were common.

So when the first Garden Walk Buffalo, the city's free, self-guided tour of residential gardens, debuted in 1995, Dorritie saw an opportunity for regeneration on her tucked-away block. She and other neighbors joined forces and went knocking on doors up and down the street, encouraging neighboring homeowners to start their own gardens. She even submitted Garden Walk applications on their behalf. Her plan took root and put Little Summer Street on the map.

Today, thousands flock to the block every Garden Walk weekend during the last weekend of July. But you can visit any time during the growing season to see this charming street and experience this neighborhood's regeneration in full bloom.

Address Summer Street between York Street & Richmond Avenue, Buffalo, NY 14222 | Getting there Bus 19, 22 to Summer Street & Richmond Avenue | Hours Unrestricted | Tip Walk among the thousands of annuals at the Erie Basin Marina's Trial Gardens, which serve as a testing ground for seed companies from around the world (329 Erie Street, www.visitbuffaloniagara.com/businesses/the-gardens-at-erie-basin-marina).

62 Love Canal Neighborhood

Forgotten community with a toxic past

It's a place that most Western New Yorkers would prefer to forget: a nearly abandoned Niagara Falls neighborhood that was the site of one of the country's worst environmental disasters.

There are no road signs notifying visitors that they've arrived at Love Canal. On the edge of the city along Colvin Boulevard, the houses begin to thin out, and a fence encircling a massive field filled with monitoring equipment appears. Beyond it, whole city blocks where a neighborhood once thrived sit abandoned, except for a few homes along 101st and 102nd Streets. Streetlights still line the empty roads, and vegetation grows where houses once stood. Every few hundred feet, a yellow fire hydrant appears, ready to prevent an inferno, while the real disaster that destroyed this community seeped from underground.

Long before this was a neighborhood, businessman William Love began to dig a canal here during the 19th century with the dream of building a "Model City." But he abandoned the project ultimately. Hooker Chemical eventually used the partially dug canal as a dumping ground for drums of toxic waste, then covered it, and sold it to the city in the 1950s. A neighborhood was then developed on the site. But the chemicals began to leech into the houses and schools built there, sickening residents and causing a public uproar in the 1970s. The federal government eventually evacuated and razed much of the neighborhood, and capped the toxic landfill.

A small memorial on 93rd Street recalls these events. It's worth considering that the relentless activism of Lois Gibbs and other neighborhood residents ultimately inspired the legislation that created the Environmental Protection Agency's Superfund program. Drive through this forgotten neighborhood to see firsthand the scars left behind and the haunting lessons from one of the darkest chapters in the region's history.

Address 93rd to 102nd Streets between Colvin Boulevard and Frontier Avenue, Niagara Falls, NY 14304; Memorial: 1059 93rd Street, Niagara Falls, NY 14304 | Getting there By car, take Lasalle Expressway E to Williams Road N, then left on Colvin Boulevard | Hours Unrestricted | Tip Discover another abandoned site at Lockport's Union Station, which has remained a burned-out ruin since a fire destroyed the brick structure in the 1970s (95 Union Street, Lockport).

63__The Mark Twain Room
The original manuscript of a literary masterpiece

Walk towards the nonfiction shelves in downtown's Central Library, and you'll discover a small room which contains artifacts so extraordinary that they almost seem fictional. The library converted its former smokers' lounge into the Mark Twain Room in 1995 – a small exhibition space dedicated to the author, who worked in this city as a newspaper editor in the early 1870s. At the center of the room, encased in glass, is the original manuscript of Twain's 1884 masterpiece, *The Adventures of Huckleberry Finn*, displayed two pages at a time.

The manuscript's journey to Buffalo is worthy of its own novel. Some 15 years after living here, Twain received a letter from Buffalo attorney and library curator James Gluck, who requested he donate the manuscript of the recently released book. Twain obliged but only sent half of the manuscript, believing the other half had been destroyed in a fire. But then an incredible discovery in 1991 changed the story: the second half of the manuscript appeared inside a trunk in Hollywood! It turned out that Twain had sent the other half of the manuscript to Gluck after finding it the following year, but Gluck never shared it before his unexpected death. The manuscript followed Gluck's family to their new home in California, where his granddaughters attempted to auction it off.

The library stepped in, and, after months of litigation, successfully laid claim to the other half of the manuscript, reuniting Twain's work and opening the room dedicated to him several years later. Hundreds of Twain's books and other memorabilia line the shelves surrounding the original manuscript, from dozens of foreign language editions of *Huckleberry Finn* to a Twain-branded box of cigars – and even the original wooden mantelpiece from his Delaware Avenue home, which later burned down. This small, wood-paneled room is a must-visit shrine for Twain fans.

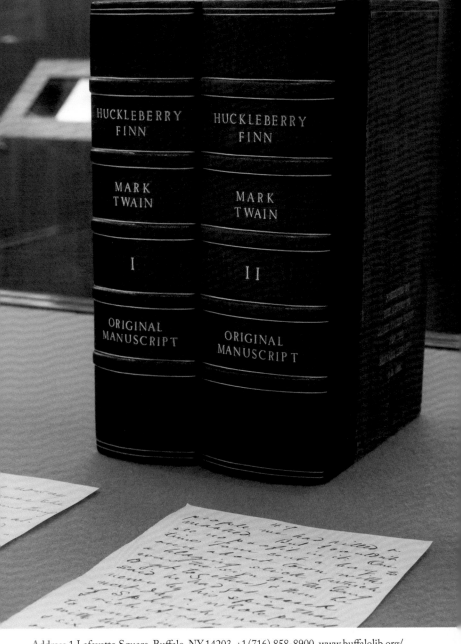

Address 1 Lafayette Square, Buffalo, NY 14203, +1 (716) 858-8900, www.buffalolib.org/locations-hours/central-downtown-buffalo | **Getting there** Metro Rail to Evans Bank @ Lafayette Square; bus 1, 4, 6, 8, 14 to Ellicott & William Streets | **Hours** Mon–Thu 8am–7pm, Fri & Sat 9am–5pm, Sun noon–5pm | **Tip** An enormous mural by Brazilian artist Eduardo Kobra depicts Twain and his friend John T. Lewis, who may have been the inspiration for the character of Jim in *Huckleberry Finn* (1188 Hertel Avenue).

64 The Martin House

Art glass windows of an architectural genius

For a window into Frank Lloyd Wright's genius, look no further than the hundreds of pieces of complex and beautiful art glass he designed for Buffalo's Martin House.

Nearly 450 art glass windows and doors blur the boundary between the inside and outside of several buildings that Wright built on this 1.5-acre campus that includes the Martin House, Barton House, Gardener's Cottage and Conservatory. The windows contain up to 750 individual pieces of colorful glass and connect with the lush landscapes he designed on the surrounding grounds. Wright produced 16 different art glass patterns found throughout the property, from the iconic "Tree of Life" windows that provide views of the verdant front yard, to the wisteria design in the Martin House's dining room that overlooks the vines growing outside. On sunny days, the windows cast a colorful prism across the Martin House's rooms and reflect shades of green, yellow, and orange as the seasons change. Wright designed the windows to enrich people's experience as they looked outside.

The intricate window designs reveal the strong relationship Wright had with Buffalo industrialist Darwin Martin, who gave the architect creative license to build an early career masterwork. While much of the original art glass remained after the Martin family abandoned the complex in 1937, some eventually landed in the hands of public and private collections. A multi-decade, multimillion-dollar restoration and reconstruction of the campus included replicating lost pieces of art glass and tracking down originals that had scattered across the continent. Museums as far away as Denver and Vancouver have returned original windows to the Martin House, and one local man even brought back a piece that he found on the ground as a boy. The art glass sheds light on the rise, fall, and reclamation of one of Buffalo's most important architectural landmarks.

Address 125 Jewett Parkway, Buffalo, NY 14214, +1 (716) 856-3858, www.martinhouse.org, info@martinhouse.org | Getting there Bus 8 to Main Street & Jewett Parkway, walk two blocks west | Hours See website for tour schedule | Tip Drive along the lakeshore to explore Graycliff, another restored Frank Lloyd Wright gem, which the architect created as a summer home for the same Martin family (6472 Old Lakeshore Road, Derby, www.experiencegraycliff.org).

65 The Monocle

A department store for a new generation

Inside a former Hertel Avenue synagogue, you can shop for furniture, books, and clothing, grab a haircut, and order a drink at the city's first department store in a generation.

The Monocle is a throwback to the days when Buffalonians once enjoyed shopping and dining in downtown's bustling department stores. Its spacious, bright upper floor – the synagogue's former worship space – features Room, an interior design and furniture store that also sells housewares, jewelry, and clothing. Downstairs, patrons wander between Crockett & Co., a barber shop that serves complimentary drinks with every shave and haircut; The Library, a cozy seating area and extension of Room, where every book on the shelf and piece of furniture is for sale; and Mister Pots, an eight-seat cocktail bar.

Interior designer Michael Poczkalski and his partner David Brugh opened The Monocle in 2022, after researching similar concepts in New York and London. "I don't like it when retailers don't step up and create a beautiful space," Poczkalski said. "We've gotten away from that. We need to get back into a community zone where betterment for all is the key."

Poczkalski recalled taking the bus downtown as a child with his grandmother to shop and eat at AM&A's department store. He wanted to recreate that experience for a new generation. The Monocle's merchandise reflects the tastes and travels of its owners, such as German coffee cups, Scandinavian watering cans, Italian lamps, books about European menu design and Panamanian hats, candles from Denmark, vases from Portugal, and animal pottery from the UK. Poczkalski wants his guests to pull up a chair, linger, and then leave feeling inspired. He and Brugh may have solved the riddle of how to lure online shoppers back into brick-and-mortar stores by creating an unforgettable experience that keeps them coming back.

Address 1235 Hertel Avenue, Buffalo, NY 14216, www.themonoclebuffalo.com, info@themonoclebuffalo.com | **Getting there** Bus 11, 23 to Hertel & Commonwealth Avenues | **Hours** See website | **Tip** Drive out to Lancaster to shop at one of the region's oldest clothing stores, The New York Store, which has been a mainstay in the village since 1929 (16 Central Avenue, Lancaster, www.new-york-store.com).

66 My Cuzin Vintage
Old school sports gear for Buffalo's biggest fans

Inside an Allentown shop, hundreds of decades-old T-shirts, hats, and coats for sale that formerly filled the closets of Buffalo sports fans have become some of the city's hottest buys.

My Cuzin Vintage is a go-to destination for anyone looking to fill out their wardrobe with reminders of the city's proud sports history. Along the racks and shelves of this small store, shoppers can find shirts with the Sabres 1990s "Goathead" logo, tees with quarterback Jim Kelly's yearly stats from 1986 to 1990, Zubaz pants, officially licensed Bills slipper socks, and baseball jackets featuring Buster Bison's likeness. Fans of the long-lost Buffalo Blizzard Major League soccer team, the short-lived Buffalo Destroyers arena football team, and the Buffalo Braves basketball franchise might stumble upon rare merchandise. My Cuzin Vintage has even sold off 30-year-old bottles of Bills-branded sunscreen, Scotch tape, and bars of soap; commemorative Super Bowl beer cups; and boxes of T.O.s Honey Toasted Oats, the cereal named after wide receiver Terrell Owens' short-lived stint here.

It should come as no surprise that a store like this has thrived in a city that lives and breathes sports. "We've got the best fans in the NFL," co-owner Vince Spano said. "It actually makes a difference in our lives if they win or lose. We don't brush it off." Spano, a former Buffalo public school gym teacher and 17-year Bills season ticket holder, first conceived of the shop after posting much of his personal sports memorabilia collection on social media. His followers asked if he'd ever consider selling his collection, which inspired him to start a side hustle online, then open a store with co-owner Derrek Hoffman in 2015. The pair have scoured flea markets, garage sales, and website forums to fill the shop with merchandise that speaks to the collective memories of Buffalo's passionate fan base.

Address 168 Elmwood Avenue, Buffalo, NY 14201, +1 (716) 322-0647, www.mycuzinvintage.com, mycuzinvintage@gmail.com | Getting there Bus 19, 20 to Elmwood Avenue & North Street | Hours Mon–Fri noon–8pm, Sat 11am–8pm, Sun 11am–5pm | Tip Continue your vintage shopping spree at Oxford Pennant, which ships vintage-themed pennants made on-site downtown to cities, sports teams, and other organizations across the continent (731 Main Street, www.oxfordpennant.com).

67 — The Nash House

A spiritual leader and pillar of the community

It's no coincidence that the last house standing on a street called Nash is a residence bearing the same name. The Nash House on Nash Street was the longtime home of the Rev. J. Edward Nash, pastor of the Michigan Street Baptist Church and a pillar of Buffalo's Black community. Nash first took to the pulpit at the church in 1892 and remained there until 1953. To put his tenure in perspective, the Supreme Court upheld segregation in the Plessy vs. Ferguson case shortly after Nash began preaching, and then integrated schools in Brown vs. the Board of Education the year after he retired. The reverend helped advance Civil Rights in Buffalo, inviting luminaries like Booker T. Washington to speak and helping found the Buffalo Urban League.

The Nash House, which Nash and his wife first moved into in 1925, is a meticulously preserved house museum that reflects a man who practiced what he preached, according to docent Sharon Holley. Many of the Nash family's household items remain, from the reverend's study filled with his papers to the 1917 Victrola the family played and the stove Francis Nash first cooked on. "Most people, when they come to Buffalo, want to see the mansions on Delaware Avenue," Holley said. "This is a lived-in home of a family who didn't have much. But they did take care of what they did have."

Nash's wife, 30 years his junior, would live at the house into the 1980s. As urban renewal brought down every other home on Nash Street (renamed after the reverend in the 1950s), Mrs. Nash fought diligently to keep her house – and her husband's legacy – alive. The Nash family hardly touched the inside through the decades, leading preservationists to discover a nearly untouched abode, a time capsule to another era, when they first stepped inside in 1999. This house and the street it sits on are an enduring reminder of a man who dedicated his life to Buffalo.

Address 36 Nash Street, Buffalo, NY 14204, +1 (716) 400-2826, www.nashhousemuseum.com, nashhouse36@gmail.com | Getting there Bus 4 to Broadway & Michigan Avenue, or bus 1 to William & Nash Streets | Hours Sat 11am–4pm or by appointment | Tip Follow Nash's footsteps to the Michigan Street Baptist Church, which dates back to 1845. Nash preached here from 1892 till the early 1950s (511 Michigan Avenue, www.michiganstreetbaptistchurch.org).

68 Niagara Aerospace Museum

Rediscover the region's aviation history

"This is an innovation goldmine," Joe Bell says. "There's nothing in aerospace that hasn't happened in Western New York in terms of the core technology. When you think about what went on here, it blows your mind."

Bell is the executive director of the Niagara Aerospace Museum, which showcases the region's rich aviation history within a former airport passenger terminal on the edge of Niagara Falls. The museum features a remarkable collection of aircraft made in Western New York throughout the 20th century, including the first mass-produced plane, the first commercial helicopter, wartime fighter jets, and even 2 of the remaining 10 lunar module engines in existence from the Apollo program. There's even a fighter jet that was shot down over Russia in World War II and recovered from the bottom of a lake in 2004. And the space-age rocket belt made famous in the James Bond movie *Thunderball* is on display here.

The region led the way in American aviation because of Glen Curtiss, who built what was then the largest airplane manufacturing plant in the world on Elmwood Avenue in North Buffalo (now mostly demolished) in order to make the Jenny, the first mass-produced airplane. His ingenuity and ambition created a skilled labor pool in Buffalo and gave rise to a succession of other aviation companies here, including Curtiss-Wright and Bell Aircraft. Some 360,000 Western New Yorkers worked in aviation from 1910 to 1999 – 50,000 alone during World War II – and 10 percent of all airplanes built during that war were assembled here.

The exhibits here show the progression of flight through the 20th century and underscore why Western New York was – as Bell puts it – "the birthplace of the American aviation industry."

Address 9990 Porter Road, Niagara Falls, NY 14304, +1 (716) 297-1323,
www.niagaraaerospacemuseum.org | Getting there Bus 59 to Niagara Falls
Boulevard & NFIA | Hours Sat & Sun 11am – 4pm | Tip Just past the airport, you'll
see the long-shuttered Bell Aerospace Company hangars, which still feature the
company's signage on the front (2106 Niagara Falls Boulevard).

69 Niagara Square
Where Buffalo witnessed its only public execution

Long before hosting summer festivals and community protests, Niagara Square was the site of Buffalo's first – and last – public execution: the hanging of three brothers nearly two centuries ago.

Back in 1825, there was no City Hall along Niagara Square, no federal courthouse, no Statler Hotel, and no McKinley Monument obelisk flanked by stone lions and fountains. But the square still functioned as the heart of the village of Buffalo, which was seven years away from becoming a city. It was the logical place to host the hanging of the Thayer brothers, a spectacle that *The Buffalo News* described in 1975 as never having "quite been matched for its intensity of feeling." The trio had murdered a Lake Erie sailor named John Love, who had been boarding with them in the winter months. Israel, Isaac, and Nelson Thayer had borrowed a couple hundred dollars from Love and opted to shoot him in the back and fatally stab him rather than repay him. The murder outraged the citizens, and the brothers were sentenced to death.

Some reports estimated that 30,000 people descended upon downtown for the execution – a remarkable number given that only 24,000 lived across the entire county in the 1825 census. A military parade led the brothers from the jail at present-day Lafayette Square and down Court Street to the gallows on the edge of Niagara Square. The sheriff used a "sword of justice," now on display at The Buffalo History Museum, to slash through the gallows' ropes and send the three brothers plunging to their deaths.

The crowd reacted with "repulsion," *The News* later reported, as Buffalo was "an innocent community that had never before known a major case of crime and punishment." Buffalo, seemingly haunted by the memory, never hosted another public execution. Niagara Square today is a popular community gathering place, but it also once tested Buffalo's very limits of propriety and morality.

Address Niagara Square, intersections of Delaware Avenue, and Court, Genesee, and Niagara Streets, Buffalo, NY 14202 | Getting there Bus 1, 2, 3, 4, 5, and more to Niagara Square & City Hall | Hours Unrestricted | Tip Head to Forest Lawn Cemetery to find the gravestone of dentist Alfred Southwick, who invented another form of execution in the 1880s: the electric chair (1990 Main Street, www.forest-lawn.com).

70 The Nine-Eleven Tavern
Wings that are all in the family

At the Nine-Eleven Tavern, co-owner Paige Gress believes there is no need to complicate the menu, which has just four wing flavors – hot, medium, mild, and plain – and five different foods. Gress isn't going to expand to other flavors and "all that fancy stuff," as it wouldn't be in keeping with the South Buffalo bar that her late father Mark opened more than 40 years ago.

Not much has changed since then, from the neon beer signs and Bills' memorabilia lining the wood-paneled walls to the table shuffleboard found near the bar. Paige still arranges every order of wings just as her father did, placing the crispy flats, drums, and celery on the plate like spokes on a wagon wheel, and garnishing every bowl of blue cheese with celery leaves. Customers have told her that eating wings plated so specifically makes them feel like royalty. Her father first started preparing wings as a new source of revenue in the 1980s when his original bar clientele, steelworkers from nearby mills, lost their jobs and disappeared.

For almost four decades, he was the sole chef at the tavern, developing a secret, tangy homemade hot sauce that locals swore by and serving French fries made from freshly cut potatoes. He shared his sauce recipe with Paige, who loved following him around as a kid and learned it when she was 12. When Mark fell ill in 2020 and found out he only had weeks to live, he taught Paige everything he knew about preparing some of Buffalo's best wings in the kitchen on one July afternoon. He passed away the following month.

Paige didn't think twice about keeping her father's tavern. She has been the sole chef since his death, making sure every plate served honors his recipes, preparation style, and work ethic. "He crafted something so monumental to Buffalo. It's a constant living in his shoes," she said. "This place can't go anywhere. I really do feel that it keeps him alive."

Address 9-11 Bloomfield Avenue, Buffalo, NY 14220, +1 (716) 825-9939, www.facebook.com/
TheNineElevenTavern | Getting there Bus 16 to South Park & Crystal Avenues | Hours
Wed–Sat 4:30pm–1am | Tip Sample more of Buffalo's best wings at Elmo's Bar & Grill,
which serves "double dipped" wings that are fried, sauced, grilled, and finally tossed in a
differently flavored sauce (2349 Millersport Highway, Getzville, www.visitbuffaloniagara.com/
crawl/buffalo-wing-trail).

71 Olcott Beach Carousel Park

Bringing back your grandparents' summer fun

Inside the Olcott Beach Carousel Park, band organ music floats through the crowd as children and families queue at the decades-old ticket booth to purchase rides for a quarter each. Near the Lake Ontario shoreline, this once vacant and decaying amusement park has been brought back to life through the hard work of volunteers.

Girls and boys line up for the Herschell Sky Fighter planes, kiddie cars, rocket swings, miniature boats, a Ferris wheel, and restored carousel, most of which date back nearly a century. You can also play some of the last remaining ski ball in Western New York, take your chances in a duck pond carnival game, and have your fortune told by Esmeralda the automaton inside the park's arcade. From there, you can wander down the street to the nearby Lakeview Village Shoppes' boardwalk to enjoy an ice cream cone by the water or relax on the lakeshore at Olcott Beach.

Olcott had been a resort destination since the turn of the 20th century, but its glory days had faded decades ago, as the last of its several amusement parks closed and the sounds of the band organ faded into memory. By the time retired schoolteacher Rosemary Sansone moved there in the 1990s, all that remained of the former Olcott Amusement Park was a vacant roundhouse where the carousel once stood. She recalled seeing a grandfather share his memories of the old park with his grandson as he walked past the empty property's chain link fence and decided this lakeside village deserved better.

Sansone worked with the community to track down some of the original rides that had scattered nationwide and fundraise to relocate them back to Olcott. The Olcott Beach Carousel Park opened in 2003 and is maintained by a dedicated group of volunteers who return every summer, along with children making new lifelong memories.

Address 5979 E Main Street, Olcott, NY 14126, +1 (716) 778-7066,
www.olcottbeachcarouselpark.org | Getting there By car, take NY-270 N to NY-93 W,
turn left on Coomer Road, right onto W Lake Road, and continue on Lockport Street
Drive to East Main Street | Hours See website for seasonal hours | Tip On the drive back,
grab a hot dog and fries from Reid's Drive-in, a roadside staple in Lockport for more than
75 years (150 Lake Avenue, Lockport, www.facebook.com/reids.in).

72 The Old Chapel
Miraculous merch in a former church

Jacob Wankasky sells antiques and handcrafted items in the same space where he was baptized, went to Confession, and made his First Communion decades earlier.

Wankasky is the co-owner of The Old Chapel Antique & Artisan Market, which features more than 150 vendors selling thousands of pieces of merchandise, from furniture and decor to collectibles and jewelry, inside a repurposed North Tonawanda Catholic church. Shoppers browse for fine china inside the church's former confessional and shop for candles in the old "crying room," where mothers could take their fussing children so as not to disrupt the services. Scores of unique finds fill the church basement, like *Star Wars* action figurines, vinyl records, stereo receivers, and a 1970s illuminated bar sign advertising Schlitz beer.

Patrons can grab a cup of coffee from the market's café and walk upstairs to the former choir loft, which still features the old church's original pipe organ and looks out over the chapel's stained-glass windows. Most vendors don't staff their areas and only rent a shelf or two, which opens up The Old Chapel to a wide variety of sellers.

Wankasky and his wife Jennifer first started selling antiques as a side hustle before opening their own shop in 2017. They quickly outgrew that space and were looking for a new home when Jacob heard that his childhood church was up for sale. Ascension was North Tonawanda's first Catholic church when it opened in the 1890s and held more than a century's worth of Sunday services before its closure in 2007. Jacob's parents and grandparents had attended the church before him, and he spent his childhood years at religious education classes in the basement. His interest in re-energizing his childhood church created one of Western New York's most extraordinary shopping experiences and gave new life to this beautiful old house of worship.

Address 172 Robinson Street, North Tonawanda, NY 14120, +1 (716) 545-6102, www.facebook.com/TheOldChapelMarket | Getting there Bus 25 to Oliver & Robinson Streets, walk two blocks east | Hours Daily 10am – 6pm | Tip Continue browsing for unique collectibles at Antique World in Clarence Hollow, the region's largest antique center and flea market that features more than 200 antique dealers (11111 Main Street, Clarence, www.antiqueworldmarket.com).

73 Old Fort Niagara
Retracing the steps of a war heroine

Inside the attic of Old Fort Niagara's 300-year-old French Castle, visitors can pay their respects to a War of 1812 heroine who is finally getting her due.

Nowhere else in Western New York quite compares to the fort, which features a centuries-old castle, powder magazine, bake house, and several other historic structures set on 250 acres along Lake Ontario. The French, British, and Americans all battled to control this fort in the 18th and 19th centuries. It was during the last of these conflicts, the War of 1812, that American Betsy Doyle rolled up her sleeves to help defeat the British. Doyle, a laundress and nurse at the fort, assisted American soldiers as they traded cannon shots with British-held Fort George across the Niagara River in Canada. She carried iron cannonballs heated to a cherry red 1,000 degrees from a fireplace on the lower levels of the fort's castle up a winding stairwell to the top floor where the cannons lay.

Perhaps grief and revenge motivated Doyle, as British soldiers had captured her husband Andrew, an artillerist, in Canada that fall. The lieutenant colonel commander of the fort, George Feeley, commended Doyle for displaying "fortitude equal to the Maid of Orleans."

"She wasn't going to be put down or allowed some subservient role," Old Fort Niagara Executive Director Bob Emerson said. "She did all she could with what she had at moments of crisis."

Doyle fled across the state prior to the fort's capture by the British in December of 1813, and died near Albany several years later without receiving compensation from the US government – or reuniting with her husband. Fort officials pieced together her story and commemorated her with a plaque in the castle's attic during the war's bicentennial celebration. A trip up to the castle's top floor is a must when visiting the fort to honor this once-forgotten figure.

Address 102 Morrow Plaza, Youngstown, NY 14174, +1 (716)-745-7611, www.oldfortniagara.org, info@oldfortniagara.org | Getting there By car, I-190 N to Niagara Scenic Parkway, exit toward NY-18F/Fort Niagara, continue to the fort | Hours See website for seasonal hours | Tip Head to nearby Artpark to find the plaque commemorating the first French settlement that preceded Old Fort Niagara: the long-gone Magazin Royal, which dated back to 1720 (450 S 4th Street, Lewiston, www.artpark.net).

74 __ Our Lady of Seneca Street

Say a prayer at this neighborhood shrine

Nestled among breweries, loft apartments, and restaurants in Buffalo's buzzy Larkinville neighborhood is a 15-foot-tall shrine to the Virgin Mary. Buffalonians have turned to this shrine for divine intercession for decades, slipping handwritten prayers and photos of loved ones into the mail slot of the small structure that features multiple religious statues, rosaries, and a large painting of Mary along the back wall. Some of the notes placed inside the shrine implore for help in finding a new job, while others ask for assistance in battling mental health issues.

Even as the surrounding area has filled with food truck rodeos and live music, the shrine has endured as a reminder of the neighborhood's past. Barber Louis Battaglia, who lived and worked next door, built it in 1955 after experiencing a vision of the Virgin Mary on three separate occasions. "She came to me to notify the people of the world to stop fighting," Battaglia once wrote in a prayer card. "I hope the President will hear the message ... and if he did not read about my little Shrine, I hope he will read and listen to my appeal quickly." Battaglia left the shrine after his death in the care of his neighbors on Seneca Street, who have continued to maintain it since.

Luis Battista, who lives across the street, has been its caretaker since the early 1990s. He uses the donations placed in the mail slot – mostly $1 or $5, but he received $50 once – to pay for the modest electrical bills accrued from illuminating the shrine each night. "I promised I would take care of it as long as I live," Battista said. The Catholic Church has never officially recognized the shrine in its nearly 70-year existence. But this small site is still worth a visit both to remember the devotion of the barber who built it and the close-knit neighborhood that continues to make sure his legacy lives on.

Address 847 Seneca Street, Buffalo, NY 14210 | Getting there Bus 15 to Seneca & Hydraulic Streets | Hours Unrestricted | Tip Spend an afternoon at the sprawling Our Lady of Fatima Shrine near Lewiston, which features an "avenue of saints," a giant rosary, and even a waterfall (1023 Swann Road, Youngstown, www.fatimashrine.com).

75___Our Lady
of Victory Basilica
2,500 angels adorn this heavenly church

For a glimpse of heaven on earth, enter Our Lady of Victory Basilica (OLV), walk down its aisle, and look up at its extraordinary dome.

This basilica, which rivals the grandest cathedrals in Europe, includes pews made with African mahogany, a replica of the Lourdes grotto sourced from Pompeii volcanic rock, 46 types of marble, and 2,500 depictions of angels scattered throughout. But perhaps no detail is as breathtaking as the basilica's dome, hailed as one of the largest in the country at the time of its completion. Its 82-foot circumference soars 170 feet above guests and features another 80-foot gap between the ceiling and its copper exterior. The dome's mural depicts dozens of angels and saints welcoming Mary, the mother of Jesus, into heaven. Italian Artist Gonippo Raggi found inspiration for the dome at the nearby Our Lady of Victory Infant Home, painting the faces of babies he saw there onto the angels depicted on the mural.

The basilica's founder, the Rev. Nelson Baker, wanted visitors to be deeply moved when they walked inside, according to the current pastor, the Rev. Msgr. David LiPuma. "He wanted people to have an experience that there's more to this world than we can see," LiPuma said. OLV was the culmination of Baker's lifelong devotion to Mary, which began when he visited Paris' Basilique Notre-Dame-des-Victoires as a young seminarian. Baker became known as the "patron of direct mail," creating a network of tens of thousands of donors nationwide whose contributions helped build a hospital, infant home, orphanage, and the basilica in Lackawanna. A small museum downstairs shares more about the life and legacy of Baker, who is entombed inside the grotto. Whether religious or not, it's worth visiting this architectural wonder to marvel at what one man's convictions created over the course of a lifetime.

Address 767 Ridge Road, Lackawanna, NY 14218, +1 (716) 828-9444, www.olvbasilica.org, olvrectory@ourladyofvictory.org | **Getting there** Bus 16, 42 to Ridge Road & South Park Avenue | **Hours** Sun–Fri 6:30am–7pm, Sat 6:30am–7:30pm | **Tip** Walk over to the Buffalo and Erie County Botanical Gardens to see thousands of flowers and plants under the tri-domed glass conservatory designed by Lord & Burnham, an architectural firm that started in Buffalo in 1849 (2655 South Park Avenue, www.buffalogardens.com).

76 Penn-Dixie Fossil Reserve

Ancient fossil treasures at your fingertips

With a garden trowel in one hand and a bucket in another, you can visit a former Blasdell quarry to sift through mounds of rocks and find 380-million-year-old fossils. It takes several minutes after arriving at Penn-Dixie Fossil Park to train your eye and distinguish rock from fossil. But then the tiny snails, clams, coral, and other creatures that lived here when this land was part of a tropical ocean south of the equator come into focus.

As the earth's tectonic plates moved at about the rate that fingernails grow, the sea eventually reached Western New York's present latitude 43 degrees north of the equator. Melting glaciers at the end of the Ice Age millions of years later brought these ancient invertebrates close to the surface. "Tell anybody that they're digging for things older than dinosaurs, and it kind of blows their mind," Associate Director Dr. Holly Schreiber said. "You're guaranteed to find a fossil unless you're not even looking at the ground."

The Penn-Dixie Cement Company mined this land for nearly 20 years as a rock quarry, digging just far enough to expose the fossils. After the quarry shut down in the 1970s, locals used the abandoned lot as a hangout for teenage parties and a dumping ground for tires and other household waste. It wasn't until the 1990s that a group of local geologists joined with concerned community members to form a non-profit to create the park, one of only a few across the US where visitors can take fossils home with them.

The 54-acre park features several acres of rock mounds, where visitors can search for approximately 10,000 fossils that remain on the property. Dr. Schreiber estimates that it will take at least another century before Penn-Dixie exhausts its fossil supply – plenty of time for visitors to enjoy it, but a mere drop (or fossil) in the bucket compared to the long history of this extraordinary site.

Address 4050 North Street, Blasdell, NY 14219, +1 (716) 627-4560, www.penndixie.org | Getting there By car, take Route 5 S to Big Tree Road to Bristol Avenue and follow the signs | Hours See website for seasonal hours | Tip Shop for ancient fossils and meteorite fragments at the nearby Past & Present Science and Nature Store, which also features a free exhibit of dinosaur bones and other specimens (3767 South Park Avenue, Blasdell, www.pastpres.com).

77 Prophet Isaiah's House

The colorful story behind this elaborate home

Western New York's most colorful home might just be a small abode on a quiet Niagara Falls street that will soon be reborn as a community center and museum.

To say that the Second Coming House of Prophet Isaiah stands out from the rest of the homes on Ontario Street would be an understatement. As motorists drive past homes with brick façades and beige or gray vinyl siding, a bungalow featuring every color of the rainbow comes into view. Dozens of painted crosses, stars, and other religious iconography cover nearly every inch of its exterior, from the front steps and the door to the roof trim. Hundreds of hand-drawn geometric shapes create a rich visual mosaic.

This work of art was the home of Isaiah Robertson, a carpenter by trade and native of Jamaica who moved to Niagara Falls nearly three decades ago. Robertson's house and front yard became his canvas for expressing his religious convictions, according to Ally Spongr, director of public art for the Niagara Falls National Heritage Area. At one time, an elaborate sculpture filled with similar imagery, which Robinson took years to build, stood alongside the house. "He was driven by visions from God, and that experience drove him to create," Spongr said. "He felt he needed to share these messages with the world, and he used his art to be able to do that."

Robertson passed away in 2020, leaving the house's future in question. His wife, Ms. Gloria, sold it to the Kohler Foundation, which has since removed and conserved the original artwork next to the house. The heritage area is working with the foundation to repurpose the home into a community gathering space and museum that will feature Robertson's original artwork, while replica pieces will be re-installed outside. Their efforts will keep visitors coming to the Prophet Isaiah's home to learn about Robertson's life, legacy, and extraordinary artistic ability.

Address 1308 Ontario Avenue, Niagara Falls, NY 14305 | Getting there Bus 52 to Ontario Avenue, walk two blocks west | Hours Unrestricted from the outside | Tip Admire more of Isaiah Robertson's legacy in the woodwork he created within the sanctuary of Mount Erie Baptist Church (1152 Fairfield Avenue, Niagara Falls).

78__The Riviera Theatre
How they saved the Mighty Wurlitzer

Before every concert at the Riviera Theatre, patrons pack the nearly century-old auditorium for an opening act to hear the mighty Wurlitzer theater organ. This is the sound of North Tonawanda.

The organist strikes the Wurlitzer's dozens of keys, pedals, and stop tabs to bring the 3,000 pipes concealed behind the theater's walls to life and fill the expansive venue with thunderous music. Medleys of Disney songs, movie themes, and other familiar favorites delight the crowd. Other buttons on the organ create sound effects that formerly accompanied movies in the silent era, including waves on the beach, the clip-clop of horses' hooves, the clash of a gong, and a train whistle. The 1926 theater organ is one of only 30 left in the United States that remain in the place where they were originally installed, and the last one still operating in North Tonawanda, which manufactured them for generations at the nearby Wurlitzer plant.

"To imagine that people 100 years ago could think of how to make all those sounds with one person playing it is absolutely phenomenal," Riviera Theatre board member Neil Lange said. "This is a piece of living history." Lange credits the Wurlitzer with saving the historic theater in the heart of North Tonawanda, which had fallen on hard times by the 1980s. The Niagara Frontier Theater Organ Society purchased the Riviera in 1989 after recognizing that the venue's demise would also destroy the Wurlitzer organ and an important piece of the city's heritage.

Wurlitzer's manufacturing plant in North Tonawanda had closed more than a decade earlier after generations in business, and the colorful theater organ remained the last link to the city's proud tradition of producing them. The society gradually restored both the theater and its organ to ensure that future generations could still enjoy the music that helped build a city.

Address 67 Webster Street, North Tonawanda, NY 14120, +1 (716) 692-2413, www.rivieratheatre.org | Getting there Bus 25 to Main & Goundry Streets | Hours See website for show schedule | Tip Grab a cold beer afterwards inside Woodcock Brothers' North Tonawanda Brewery, located inside the converted former Wurlitzer plant (908 Niagara Falls Boulevard, www.woodcockbrothersbrewery.com).

79__Rohr Hill Road

Otherworldly sculptures in the countryside

Along a country road tucked into the rolling hills of the Southern Tier, several 20-foot-tall sculptures appear on the horizon, the only occupants of otherwise uninhabited meadows and forests. Motorists driving down Rohr Hill Road will first notice towering sentinels seemingly standing guard over the empty pavement. On a field to the right, a bishop forged in steel performs a wedding ceremony for a king and queen. Visitors who wander nature trails further down the hill into the forest will discover a giant crab, a rhinoceros, a giraffe, and other creatures as well.

In this section of Griffis Sculpture Park, which is separated from the larger portion most locals know, there are no surrounding buildings, no grand entrances, and no sounds, other than the wind rustling through the trees and the buzz of crickets in the summer. This pristine greenspace filled with whimsical sculptures remains just as the late artist Larry Griffis left it more than a generation ago.

"There's very few experiences that you stumble on. Nothing is undiscovered," Griffis' granddaughter Nila Griffis Lampman says. "Rohr Hill still has that undiscovered land and undiscovered art that you're stumbling upon for the very first time."

Larry Griffis first purchased this bucolic, 100-acre property in the 1960s after gaining recognition for sculptures he had assembled at the top of Kissing Bridge's ski slopes. Rohr Hill presented the first opportunity for the former hosiery factory owner and World War II veteran to strike out on his own and bring his vision for a sculpture park to life. Griffis would soon expand into the larger Mill Valley Road site a short drive away that's far more visited today. But Griffis' original, off-the-beaten-path park with an unlisted address remains perhaps the best place to experience the otherworldly legacy of this extraordinary sculptor.

Address Rohr Hill Road, Ashford Hollow, NY 14171, +1 (716) 667-2808, www.griffissculpturepark.org | Getting there By car, take US 219 S to Plato Road | Hours Unrestricted | Tip Enjoy a Lake Erie sunset while admiring another one of Larry Griffis' sculptures, *Round Man*, which was installed in 2022 along Buffalo's Outer Harbor (Greenway Nature Trail, www.buffalowaterfront.com/outer-harbor).

80 Roosevelt Inaugural Site

Where Teddy Roosevelt took the presidential oath

Buffalo has one of the only sites where a US President took the oath of office outside the nation's capital – a history-altering moment born out of a national tragedy.

The eyes of the world turned to a stately, 19th-century house along Delaware Avenue in September of 1901 when Theodore Roosevelt became the 26th president of the United States. The occasion inside Ansley Wilcox's home library was not a joyous one. Just 14 hours earlier, Roosevelt's predecessor, President William McKinley, had died in the Milburn home on Delaware Avenue, succumbing to an assassin's bullet that struck him eight days earlier at the city's Pan-American Exposition. Roosevelt rushed here from an Adirondack hiking trip he had taken with his family.

There are only three other places in the United States outside of the nation's capital with a similar history. Calvin Coolidge became president at his family's homestead in Vermont. Chester Arthur's apartment in New York, where he took oath after President James Garfield's death, became an Indian grocery store. And the US Air Force Museum in Dayton, Ohio holds the Air Force One, where Lyndon Johnson was sworn in as commander-in-chief after John F. Kennedy's assassination.

Roosevelt had to figure out quickly where to become president after arriving in Buffalo. He shied away from the Milburn home, where McKinley's body continued to lay upstairs. Some of his cabinet members mistakenly headed to the Buffalo Club, believing that to be the inaugural site. The Roosevelt team settled on the home of Roosevelt's longtime acquaintance, Ansley Wilcox, where the president-in-waiting was already staying. Now a National Historic Site, the home has recreated the spaces where this history happened and introduced interactive exhibits that put visitors in Roosevelt's shoes as he navigated the country through a tumultuous period.

Address 641 Delaware Avenue, Buffalo, NY 14202, +1 (716) 884-0095, www.trsite.org | **Getting there** Bus 11, 12, 25 to Delaware Avenue & North Street | **Hours** Tours Mon – Fri 9am – 5pm, Sat & Sun noon – 5pm | **Tip** Discover another presidential history site at the Millard Fillmore House, which the 13th president built during the years he lived in East Aurora prior to his political rise (24 Shearer Avenue, East Aurora, www.aurorahistoricalsociety.com).

81 The Royalton Ravine

Stomping grounds of an American trailblazer

Exploring the Royalton Ravine is an adventure unlike any other – a trek complete with a long suspension bridge, mysterious ruins, and a connection to a trailblazing woman.

When you first arrive at the 146-acre park, you'll cross an expansive field before entering a forest and picking up a trail that guides you down a ravine and along the rushing waters of 18-Mile Creek. Before long, hikers reach an 80-foot-long, wooden-plank suspension bridge that crosses the waterway. Those feeling mischievous can try and knock their hiking partners off balance by jumping up and down on the wobbling bridge, which the Youth Conservation Corps built back in 1975. The trail then proceeds to a small waterfall. Look for a pile of stone ruins that have long been rumored to be the homestead of Belva Lockwood, a 19th-century trailblazer and Niagara County native who became one of the country's first female lawyers and presidential candidates. Lockwood lived in the area before moving with her husband to Washington, DC to pursue her legal career. She ran for president in 1884 and 1888.

The first references to Lockwood living in the ruins originated in the 1980s, nearly two decades after the park's creation. Some local maps online even called the area of the park the "Lockwood Ruins." But after poring over maps and property deeds from her lifetime, Niagara County Deputy Historian Craig Bacon has never found proof that Lockwood actually lived there. Instead, an adjacent property owned by her husband's family was the more likely site of her residence.

Even if Lockwood didn't live by the cascade, she almost certainly explored the same forests and creek that the park's visitors enjoy today. The ruins' true origin story remains to be discovered – adding to the intrigue of this one-of-a-kind hiking trail that has become a favorite of outdoor enthusiasts and history buffs alike.

Address 4662 Gasport Road, Gasport, NY 14207, +1 (716) 439-7951, www.niagaracounty.com/parks | Getting there By car, take NY-31 to Gasport Road | Hours Daily 7am–9pm | Tip Take another hike along the Niagara River at the Stella Niagara Preserve, which features trails that pass by a chapel and grotto built by the Sisters of Saint Francis (4214-4448 Lower River Road, Lewiston, www.wnylc.org/stella-niagara-preserve).

82 The Roycroft Inn

An Arts-and-Crafts masterpiece welcomes you

When you step into the Roycroft Inn, you're surrounded by furniture, stained glass, and murals made generations ago by a community of artisans who worked right across the street. The inn doubles as a living museum dedicated to the American Arts and Crafts movement. Handcrafted items fill nearly every space, from an elaborate stained-glass chandelier in the dining room to bookshelves, chairs, and tables branded with the letter R to mark their authenticity as actual works by Roycroft artisans.

Near the front desk, you will see elaborate murals designed by Roycroft artist Alex Fournier illustrating the eight intellectual centers of the world, including a depiction of the Roycroft Campus, the group of campus buildings across from the inn. The campus generated national buzz more than a century ago by employing craftspeople who specialized in woodworking, metalsmithing, printing, and other trades. It attracted luminaries like Henry Ford, Booker T. Washington, and Susan B. Anthony, who came here to share their like-minded ideals with Roycroft founder Elbert Hubbard and his community.

Hubbard started a print shop back in 1897 inside the inn's present-day lounge. It was from here that Hubbard printed *A Message for Garcia*, an essay extolling the virtues of hard work that sold millions of copies. He leveraged his newfound fame and fortune to build the campus and expand into other trades. Hubbard then repurposed and expanded the old print shop into the inn and filled it with goods made at the campus to remind his guests of all they could buy during their visit.

Staying overnight or grabbing brunch on the breezy peristyle transports visitors back to this era. The campus, which ceased production during the Great Depression, has since been restored, and the inn has endured as the best-preserved example from this unique era of American manufacturing.

Address 40 S Grove Street, East Aurora, NY 14052, +1 (716) 652-5552, www.roycroftinn.com,
info@roycroftinn.com | Getting there By car, take NY-400 S to Maple Street, turn left on
S Grove Street | Hours Daily 9am – 10pm | Tip Across the street, you can browse for items
made by Roycroft artisans at Roycroft Campus Antiques, a mainstay in East Aurora for more
than 50 years (37 S Grove Street, www.roycroftantiques.com).

83 Schoellkopf Power Plant

Collapsed ruins in the Niagara Gorge

Nature is reclaiming a portion of the Niagara gorge that humans once tried to conquer. Just downstream from Niagara Falls, an entirely different spectacle awaits intrepid travelers who decide to explore this quiet portion of the river: the remnants of a collapsed hydroelectric plant.

You will descend 210 feet in an elevator to the bottom of the Niagara Gorge to find the Schoellkopf Power Plant site. Twisted steel beams and stone ruins as tall as the gorge itself stand on the former location of the plant. Birds chirp, trees grow, and foxes scamper where huge turbines once powered the city of Niagara Falls. "At Schoellkopf, it's this moment of serenity. The water feels so calm at this point," says Angelina Weibel, education coordinator for the New York State Parks. "At the same time, you know there was this dramatic moment of craziness that happened and threw Niagara Falls into complete upheaval."

That moment of chaos came on June 7, 1956, when two-thirds of the power plant, constructed more than 40 years earlier, fell into the Niagara Gorge in a spectacular collapse.

That morning, workers had noticed water seeping into the plant, cracks in the walls, and bulging floors. By 5pm, a catastrophic structural failure plunged the city into darkness and killed one of the plant's foremen. Some blamed a 1946 earthquake that caused a crack along the gorge, while others maintained that the power plant's structural integrity was compromised from the get-go. The plant was gone in a matter of seconds.

For years, the only way to access the ruins was on a hiking trail that ran along the base of the gorge. That changed in 2015, when the Maid of the Mist restored the plant's original elevator shaft as part of a project to convert part of the site into storage for its fleet. Interpretive signage, easy access, and incredible views bring to life one of the most harrowing days in the history of Niagara Falls.

Address Discovery Way & Walnut Avenue, Niagara Falls, NY 14303, +1 (716) 278-1070, www.niagarafallsstatepark.com | Getting there Bus 40, 50, 77 to Main & 3rd Streets, walk four blocks | Hours See website for seasonal hours | Tip The Niagara Power Vista is a visitor center on top of the current hydro plant with incredible views and interactive exhibits about the Niagara Gorge (5777 Lewiston Road, Lewiston, www.nypa.gov/communities/visitors-centers/niagara-power-vista).

84_ Schwabl's
Buffalo's capital for beef on weck

Schwabl's may not have invented the beef on weck, Buffalo's signature sandwich, but they certainly perfected it over generations of fine tuning. This nearly 200-year-old restaurant, which the Chamber of Commerce named one of the "Pioneer Businesses of the Niagara Frontier" in 1956, might just be Buffalo's capital for beef on weck.

A neon marquee touting its roast beef, a bison statue named *Beefy*, and a "Hungry for History" plaque detailing the sandwich's origins greet customers as they arrive. Inside, co-owner Gene Staychock, clad in a white lab coat and tie, hand-carves beef to order from a 15-pound top round behind the original wooden bar. Waitresses wearing white dresses carry out plates from the kitchen, filled with generous portions of homemade German potato salad, coleslaw, and pickled beets made from recipes passed down through the decades. They stop by Staychock's station to pick up the beef on weck and then serve the meal to customers, who top their sandwiches off with sinus-clearing dollops of horseradish.

No one knows definitively when Schwabl's first started selling the beef on weck, a tender roast beef sandwich served on a hard roll studded with salt and caraway seeds. One menu dating back to the early 1900s lists roast beef as an entree. But the sandwich, which is believed to have originated in Buffalo's German taverns in the 19th century, and the restaurant, which first opened in Buffalo in 1837 before moving to West Seneca in the early 1940s, have each been a fixture for longer than anyone can remember.

Gene and his wife and co-owner Cheryl, who started working at the restaurant in 1990, ultimately purchased it from the Schwabl family and have taken great care to keep its menu, ingredients, and décor intact. "It's old-time Buffalo. It's so old fashioned. It's just tradition," Cheryl Staychock says. "Why change it if it's not broken?"

Address 789 Center Road, West Seneca, NY 14224, +1 (716) 675-2333, www.schwabls.com | Getting there By car, take NY-400 S to Union Road S | Hours Tue–Sat noon–8pm | Tip Bite into a pastry heart, a Western New York confectionery specialty, at Eileen's Centerview Bakery, a mainstay since 1964 (465 Center Road, West Seneca, https://www.eileensbakery.com).

85 The Science Museum

Rare elephant bird egg lost and then found

When a museum has collected more than 750,000 artifacts over the course of 160 years, mistakes can happen, like the mislabeling of a thousand-year-old elephant bird egg.

The Buffalo Museum of Science is one of only 40 institutions around the world to possess an intact egg from an elephant bird, which went extinct 1,000 years ago. These birds laid the largest eggs of any vertebrate animal, including dinosaurs. But the extraordinary egg inside the museum's "Rethink Extinct" exhibit sat out of public view for almost 80 years, mislabeled as a model in a behind-the-scenes glass case.

The error might have occurred around when the museum acquired the egg in 1939 from Edward Gerrard & Sons, a taxidermy shop in London renowned for its spot-on recreations, according to Kathy Leacock, the museum's deputy director. Back then, museum staff placed the mislabeled, three-and-a-half-pound egg in storage, where it had been hiding in plain sight ever since.

A breakthrough for the egg arrived several years ago, when the museum's collections manager began to clean out old storage cabinets and discovered another elephant bird egg that was clearly a model. But if that second egg was a replica, the museum's employees wondered, what then was the 1939 acquisition? Museum staff rushed the artifact in question across town to the Art Conservation Department at SUNY Buffalo State for an x-ray. The test confirmed its authenticity as a real and exceptionally rare egg from the 11-foot-tall, 1,000-pound bird that roamed the island of Madagascar centuries ago.

The museum soon shared the long-hidden egg with the public and has given it pride of place in a display ever since, alongside ostrich and hummingbird eggs to underscore its massive size. "Your collection is never complete, or static, or finished," Leacock observes. "Collections are this living, breathing thing."

Address 1020 Humboldt Parkway, Buffalo, NY 14211, +1 (716) 896-5200, www.sciencebuff.org | Getting there By car, take NY-33 to Best Street/Science Museum | Hours Daily 10am–4pm | Tip Discover more than 120 living species at the Aquarium of Niagara, including penguins, seals, jellyfish, and other marine wildlife in its exhibits (701 Whirlpool Street, Niagara Falls, www.aquariumofniagara.org).

GS **GROW?**
lps maintain the correct humidity in which
o forms a barrier that protects the embryo
nally, the shell must also be strong enough
x enough to support the weight of the parent
ficient exchange of oxygen and carbon dioxide
ping embryo. Otherwise, it would suffocate. The
rge eggs can grow – they cannot grow infinitely, and
nosaurs had smaller eggs in proportion to their size.
eighed up to 22 pounds, which is the largest an
eggs weigh in at about 3.3 pounds per egg.
nce.

ITEM: Elephant Bird Egg
Aepyornis maximus
Q. 257

STATUS: EXTINCT

DATA: Purchased 29 Dec 1939
from Edward Gerrard & Sons
[London, England]
01

ITEM: Ostrich Egg
Struthio sp.

STATUS: LEAST CONCE
TO VULNERA
02

86 Seneca Indian Park
Tread gently on this Indigenous burial ground

Buffalo's most historic property might be found a few blocks off of Seneca Street: the last remaining acre and burial ground of what was once a thriving Indigenous community. *No digging allowed* ordinances posted by the city on Buffum Street greet visitors as they approach Seneca Indian Park. The gently sloping, 1.6-acre green space features more than two dozen towering trees, some of which are centuries old. A path leading in from the street leads to a plaque on a large boulder that recalls how the Seneca Nation called this area of present-day South Buffalo home for generations in the 18th and 19th centuries.

The Seneca buried some of their most prominent residents on the property, including the orator Red Jacket, before they were removed and reburied elsewhere in the late 19th century. Another headstone marks the spot where a new set of Seneca remains were buried in the 1950s, reinterred from a portion of the Genesee Valley inundated by the construction of the Mount Morris Dam. The corner park is the final vestige of a Seneca community that thrived for generations along Buffalo Creek, now the Buffalo River.

Past archaeological digs here exhumed refuse heaps that suggest Indigenous populations lived in this area for centuries, according to an article published by the Buffalo Museum of Science in 1921. As Buffalo boomed, development encroached on those lands until all that remained was the property that contained the burial ground. Industrialist John Larkin purchased the land and deeded it to the city to become a park and historic site, a move not welcomed by the Seneca Nation.

"None of us want the feet of thousands to trample into the dust and the bones of our grandfathers and ancestors," Seneca Chief Thunderwater told *The Buffalo Courier* at the park's dedication in 1912. So treat this small park with the reverence it deserves, for this is hallowed ground.

Address 74 Fields Avenue, Buffalo, NY 14210 | Getting there Bus 15 to Seneca & Cazenovia Streets, walk to Buffum Street, make a left and walk three blocks | Hours Unrestricted | Tip Admire the basswood trees recently planted by the Western New York Land Conservancy at Red Jacket Riverfront Natural Habitat Park, honoring the Seneca name for this spot, "The Place of the Basswoods" (western end of Smith Street, www3.erie.gov/parks/red-jacket-riverfront-natural-habitat-park).

87 Seneca One Tower
Now you know what that yummy smell is

Is that Cheerios you're smelling in downtown Buffalo? Or Honey Nut Chex? Or Lucky Charms? A sign inside the city's tallest office building has solved the mystery of the toasted oat aroma that wafts through the city.

Seneca One Tower is one mile away from Buffalo's iconic General Mills factory, the nation's oldest cereal plant that has been producing Cheerios and other well-known brands along the waterfront for more than 80 years. On a good day, the southwest breezes off Lake Erie carry that aroma past the tower and far into the city's neighborhoods, making it one of Buffalo's most recognizable smells, alongside deep-fried wings and charcoal-broiled hot dogs. The tower's second-floor sign inside its public cafeteria maintains an up-to-date tracking of the specific cereals the plant produces each week.

For years, General Mills' production was a closely guarded secret, and locals could only guess which cereal the plant produced based on the aroma. Seneca One's sign removes that guesswork. Tower employees have an inside source at the plant that informs them of the specific cereal in production, and they change the sign based on that intelligence. On any given week, the *Here's What You Might Smell Downtown Today* sign might reveal Cheerios, Blueberry Cheerios, Very Berry Cheerios, Corn Chex, Honey Nut Chex, Honey Nut Cheerios, or Lucky Charms.

The sign is a nod to the sense of pride Buffalonians feel when they drive into the city and smell freshly toasted cereal, according to Joe Konze, business development associate at Seneca One. The aroma is often strongest at dawn, and stopping to smell the Cheerios is as much a part of Buffalo's culture as the Bills or blue cheese dressing, he says. "There's a sense of nostalgia that kicks up in your head when you smell that," he said. "It kind of puts a twinkle in your eye and a pep in your step."

Address 1 Seneca Street, 2nd floor, Buffalo, NY 14203, +1 (716) 314-5450,
www.senecaonebuffalo.com | Getting there Metro Rail to Seneca Street | Hours
Mon – Fri 7am – 7pm | Tip Have a Cheerios-topped waffle down the street from the General
Mills plant at Wonder Coffeehouse (323 Ganson Street, www.wondercoffeehouse.com).

88 Shea's Buffalo Theatre

Restoring greatness through dedication

Doris Collins and her team of volunteers have toiled lovingly over Shea's Buffalo Theatre for decades to restore the century-old movie palace to its former glory.

Collins has spent more than 25 years spearheading the restoration of the Theater District's crown jewel. The former art teacher and historic restoration consultant has taught a team of nearly 150 volunteers and students everything they need to know to make downtown's touring Broadway showhouse shine again. They have worked together on just about every square inch of Shea's, repairing glass chandeliers bead by bead, repainting the walls and ceiling, rehabbing original furniture and a ticket booth, and reinstalling a replica marquee, only bringing in contractors when necessary. Their efforts have saved the theater millions of dollars.

Collins' journey to find the necessary materials for the restoration even led her halfway across the world. She had been trying in vain to duplicate the theater's original drapes, when, serendipitously, an Austrian trade commission happened to walk inside the theater for a tour. Collins, having grown up in Austria, provided the tour in German and so discovered that a factory there could produce the exact same type of drapes that first graced the theater in the 1920s. She traveled there herself to make the purchase.

The former movie theater, with ornate interiors designed by Louis Comfort Tiffany, had fallen on hard times by the 1970s. Demolition rumors loomed after the city seized the building for back taxes. A grassroots effort led by a group of theater enthusiasts and an intervention by late City Comptroller George O'Connell saved Shea's, which began hosting seasons of touring Broadway shows by the 1980s. The steadfast dedication of Collins and her army of volunteers has allowed theatergoers to enjoy this magnificent venue just as Buffalo first did all those years ago.

Address 650 Main Street, Buffalo, NY 14202, +1 (716) 847-1410, www.sheas.org, patronservices@sheas.org | Getting there Bus 8, 66 to Franklin Street & Emerson Commons; Metro Rail to Fountain Plaza | Hours History tours by reservation; see website for show schedule | Tip Continue your tour of the Theater District with a show at the Irish Classical Theatre Company, which Irish brothers Vincent and Chris O'Neill founded more than 30 years ago (625 Main Street, www.irishclassical.com).

89__Silo City
Buffalo's iconic structures reimagined

On summer evenings, poets, musicians, and artists perform within the hollowed-out, 120-foot-tall interiors of a grain silo complex on Buffalo's waterfront, infusing new life into a concrete colossus.

Perhaps no other place symbolizes the story of Buffalo – its meteoric rise, post-industrial decline, and 21st-century reimagining – more than Silo City. This collection of hulking structures that once stored millions of bushels of grain along the Buffalo River has become a stomping ground for the city's vibrant and innovative creative class. Spoken word, theater, and music fill the walls of the now-empty silos at the Marine A complex, which features empty, cavernous interiors that create an incredible reverb for performances. Nearby, a former factory administration building has transformed into Duende, a craft cocktail bar filled with reclaimed materials from the silos. Urban gardens and a labyrinth bloom in previously vacant spaces, and hundreds of apartment dwellers will soon move into a former warehouse and malt house on the property.

Just 20 years ago, the scene here was much different – and far more desolate. Buffalo's days as one of the world's largest grain ports had faded away, and most of the industry that filled this property was long gone. It was Rick Smith, whose family had owned a neighboring manufacturing plant for decades, who found beauty and potential in the decay and rust. Smith purchased the complex in 2006 and eventually provided access to the 27-acre property by collaborating with other organizations, from architectural tours led by Explore Buffalo to Just Buffalo Literary Center's Silo City Reading Series. His philosophy of "slow-burn regeneration," honoring and preserving the site's authenticity through gradual redevelopment, paid off. This once barren industrial landscape has transformed into one of the most extraordinary spaces in Buffalo – and beyond.

Address 85 Silo City Row, Buffalo, NY 14203, +1 (716) 849-4780, www.silo.city, lyceumsilocity@gmail.com | Getting there Bus 42 to Ohio & Ganson Streets | Hours See website for upcoming events | Tip For unbeatable views of Buffalo's grain silos from the water, take a Buffalo River History Tour at the waterfront at Canalside (44 Prime Street, www.buffaloriverhistorytours.com).

90 — Sloan's Antiques
Step inside Buffalo's last junk shop

Max Sloan calls it, "The best kept secret in Buffalo at the end of Lonely Street." Of course, he's referring to Sloan's Antiques, his four-floor store packed to the brim with every type of antique and novelty item you could ever imagine.

Looking for a Japanese slot machine? Sloan's Antiques has it. An old hotel room radio from Buffalo's long-shuttered Genesee Hotel? A 400-year-old buffet table from Europe? A series of 1940s anima-tronic Christmas figurines from a department store window, a por-trait of Napoleon Bonaparte, an old wall menu from a Chinese restaurant, fallout shelter signs from the Cold War, or a Jolly Green Giant figure from a supermarket display? They're among the thou-sands of items lining the wooden floors of this East Side institution that's as much of a museum as it is a store.

"We don't even know everything that's in here," Sloan says. "We have so much good stuff you can't even see." Max's late father Sol, a Holocaust survivor who lost his first family in the Auschwitz concen-tration camp, opened Sloan's in 1955 after moving to the US with just a few dollars in his pocket. To make a go of it here, he returned to what he knew best from Romania, where he would use his horse-drawn peddler's wagon to collect items he later sold. Sloan's collection quickly outgrew his original store and moved into the circa 1890 William Street building that his son continues to operate today.

Sloan's has become a favorite spot for Hollywood movie crews film-ing in Buffalo and looking for props, including Reginald Hudlin's *Marshall* (2017) and Guillermo Del Toro's *Nightmare Alley* (2021). The store is one of the last remaining businesses on this mostly empty stretch of William Street – and the final old-fashioned junk shop in a city that used to be filled with them. "There's one Niagara Falls. There's one Central Terminal," Max said. "And there's one place like this."

Address 730 William Street, Buffalo, NY 14206, +1 (716) 553-5314, www.sloansantiques.com, sloansantiques@gmail.com | **Getting there** Bus 1 to William & Smith Streets | **Hours** Tue – Sat noon – 3pm | **Tip** Browse for mid-century furniture, antiques, and other oddities at CooCooU, located inside an old warehouse in Black Rock (111 Tonawanda Street, www.facebook.com/coocoou27).

91 Spare Lanes

An old bowling alley gets a new lease on life

One of downtown's newest nightlife options is right up Buffalo's alley: a set of restored, century-old bowling lanes available for rent in the basement of a Pearl Street hotel.

This tucked-away bowling alley features eight lanes that more closely resemble a sports bar or a nightclub. Flatscreen televisions at the end of each lane broadcast sporting events, and big photographic prints of the stars of "The Big Lebowski" line the walls. Neon lights straddle the sides of the lanes, which are shorter than regulation length and attract corporate events and groups of friends instead of the typical weekly competitive leagues. Visitors reach the bowling alley, which also offers a cash bar and arcade, by ascending one flight of stairs found in the Aloft hotel lobby, then descending another short stairwell. As you walk down the steps, you'll pass by a black-and-white photo that shows what Spare Lanes looked like generations ago. Back then, the venue featured wooden floors, brick columns, and signs hanging from the ceiling urging players to *WATCH YOUR STEP* and *BOWL BETTER*.

The old bowling alley was one of several gathering places inside the old Fraternal Order of Eagles Hall, which opened along Pearl Street in 1914 and created the lanes as part of an addition in 1924. The Eagles vacated the hall in the 1950s, and then The Buffalo Christian Center, which served at-risk youth for decades, converted the alley into a miniature golf course. Ellicott Development restored the lanes as part of a broader redevelopment of the building into the 500 Pearl event space and Aloft hotel in 2019.

Be sure to explore the complex's other beautifully restored banquet halls and spaces that previously served as a theater and roller rink. Spare Lanes has breathed new life into a formerly fading downtown space and reinvigorated a sport that once dominated weekend life in Buffalo.

Address 512 Pearl Street, Suite 150, Buffalo, NY 14202, +1 (716) 382-6084, www.sparelanes.com, sparelanes@ellicotthotels.com | Getting there Bus 8, 66, 81 to Pearl & Tupper Streets | Hours Wed – Sat 4pm – midnight | Tip Hit a bucket of golf balls while watching airplanes land at the Airport Driving Range, another one of the region's most unique sports experiences (207 Youngs Road, Williamsville, www.airportdrivingrange.com).

92 — Sportsmen's Tavern

Buffalo's honkiest, tonkiest music venue

In the heart of Black Rock, the nightly twang of banjos, mandolins, and acoustic guitars fills the two-floor venue known as the "Honkiest Tonkiest Beer Joint in Town." Welcome to Sportsmen's Tavern.

The Hall family has spent the better part of 40 years turning this former neighborhood watering hole into one of the city's top music destinations. Patrons file in at all hours of the day and night for lunch hour concerts and evening shows featuring local and touring bands specializing in bluegrass, folk, Americana, roots, and country music. Their melodies float from the first-floor stage to the second-floor balcony and bar made with reclaimed wood from the nearly 130-year-old building. Paintings and drawings of past acts line the tavern's wood-paneled walls, and television screens inside this music-forward venue exclusively show that night's band. Most nights, co-owner Jason Hall and other relatives tend bar and greet patrons. "No matter where you go, you're surrounded by what's happening," Hall said. "The focus is on the stage."

Sportsmen's has evolved considerably since Jason's father Dwane, a steelworker, neighborhood resident, and member of the Stone Country Band, first purchased it in 1985. Back then, the bar didn't even have a stage and attracted only nearby customers who purchased self-service cans of beer. The Halls gradually expanded the tavern and knocked out two apartments upstairs to add the second floor and expose the wooden rafters of the 1890s building. In recent years, they also converted a nearby yard into an outdoor venue known as Sportsmen's Park and adapted a former indoor archery range around the corner into another venue known as The Cave.

The burgeoning creative district, which the Halls hope to eventually brand as "Music Town," is the culmination of one family's decades-long mission to change the tune of the city they love.

Address 326 Amherst Street, Buffalo, NY 14207, +1 (716) 874-7734, www.sportsmensbuffalo.com, info@sportsmenstavern.net | Getting there Bus 32 to Amherst Street & Tops | Hours See website for showtimes | Tip For another uniquely Buffalo music experience, check out the free weekly Celtic jam sessions Saturdays at 4pm at Nietzsche's Tavern (248 Allen Street, www.nietzsches.com).

93__Stitch Buffalo

Creating opportunities one stitch at a time

Every hand-stitched and embroidered item for sale along the shelves and tables of Stitch Buffalo's retail store has a backstory that originated halfway across the world. This former Niagara Street butcher shop has been reborn as a classroom space for new arrivals from around the world to hone their stitching and embroidering skills, and as a shop to sell their products.

A Burmese woman made the hand-embroidcred earrings sold here. Another woman from Afghanistan crafted the popular hand-woven tunic. A resettled refugee from Bhutan created Stitch's peace sign pins, and natives of Nepal assembled the door hangings for sale here that are widely used in their country. Stitch sells tea towels and scarves made on-site on a backstrap loom by natives of Myanmar, and heartshaped "Buffalove" pins that have become an enduring symbol of the city's embrace of immigrants and refugees.

"We have grown so quickly out of need," Stitch Buffalo founder Dawne Hoeg said. "There's nothing else like this in the country." Since Hoeg first launched Stitch in 2014, dozens of women originally hailing from Southeast Asia, Africa, and the Middle East have developed stitching and embroidering skills here. Stitch has a tracking system that ensures a portion of every sale in the store returns to the maker. The organization also sponsors private craft parties and instruction for visitors who want to learn those same skills.

On her commute to work, Hoeg, a textiles professor at Buffalo State College, had noticed a growing number of refugee women walking in the city's West Side. She knew from her research that these women likely possessed skills from their homelands, and she wanted to launch a creative outlet for them that built on their talents. In the decade that followed, this organization has stitched together a legacy of providing economic opportunities for some of Buffalo's newest residents.

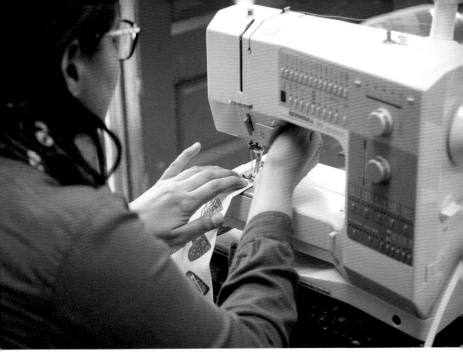

Address 1215 Niagara Street, Buffalo, NY 14213, +1 (716) 495-9642, www.stitchbuffalo.org, info@stitchbuffalo.org | Getting there Bus 5 to Breckenridge Street | Hours Mon, Fri, & Sat 10am–4pm, Wed 10am–6pm | Tip Discover a wide variety of Burmese dried goods, produce, and prepared foods at Lin Asian Market (929 Tonawanda Street).

94 __ St. Casimir Church
A future pope slept here

Buffalo's Kaisertown neighborhood features Polish taverns, Polish churches, Polish street names like Krakow, Gorski, and Pulaski – and even an immaculately preserved bedroom where the world's first Polish pope stayed nearly a half-century ago. St. Casimir Church opened a small museum inside its rectory dedicated to St. John Paul II's three-night visit here in 1976, two years before he became pope. The wood-paneled bedroom where then-Cardinal Karol Wojtyla stayed remains intact, while an adjacent sitting room has been converted into a reflection area, where visitors can kneel, pray, and attach a written prayer to the "Papal Post-It Prayer Wall."

The museum was the brainchild of St. Casimir's rector, the Rev. Czeslaw Krysa, who recalled meeting the pope during his visit. Krysa was a seminarian at the time and returned to St. Casimir's more than three decades later to lead the parish, which has a beautiful, Byzantine-style sanctuary. "The one thing you know that John Paul the Second would want is to have a place for prayer and a place for people to interact with each other," Krysa said. Stories abound from Wojtyla's visit, which was part of a larger tour of the US that he completed with a visiting Polish delegation of priests. He was known to request milk and cookies every night before going to bed, and he ordered a scotch and water at a church reception.

A commemorative plate that the future pope gifted the parish is on display in the museum. The church next door, which is absolutely stunning and worth exploring on its own, also features the vestments that Wojtyla wore to the Mass he celebrated. St. John Paul II would not return to Buffalo during his 27 years as pope. But this small museum is an enduring reminder of the lasting impression he made on the residents of Kaisertown, and of the deep and proud Polish roots in this neighborhood.

Address 160 Cable Street, Buffalo, NY 14206, +1 (716) 824-9589, www.stcasimirbuffalo.com, stcasimirbuffalo@gmail.com | Getting there Bus 2 to Clinton & Weimar Streets | Hours By appointment only | Tip St. Stanislaus is another beautiful church that dates back to 1886 and still offers masses in Polish (123 Townsend Street, www.ststansbuffalo.com).

95 — Stunters' Row

Daredevils rest in peace at Oakwood Cemetery

Even death-defying daredevils who survived a barrel ride over Niagara Falls ultimately needed a final resting place. Oakwood Cemetery, a short drive from the cataract, became their permanent residence.

Several of the most famous daredevils to ever test the Niagara's mighty waters rest near each other in a section of Oakwood known as "Stunters' Row." Annie Edson Taylor is here, who, at 62 years old, became the first person to ever go over the falls in a barrel *and survive* in 1901. Next to her is Carlisle Graham, Taylor's rival, who survived his own barrel ride through the Niagara Gorge's swirling rapids. A couple of headstones down is Captain Matthew Webb, who garnered international acclaim by successfully swimming across the English Channel, but he ultimately drowned in an attempt to swim the rapids downstream of the falls. Kirk Jones, the first person to ever survive a tumble over the falls with no protection whatsoever in 2003, rests here too after a second attempt failed in 2017.

Oakwood first opened on the edge of the city in 1851 and reserved a triangular section of its 18 acres to be known as "Stranger's Rest," a final resting place for tourists who died while visiting the falls. Over the decades, some of those visitors perished attempting stunts on the Niagara, and eventually, even those who survived daredevil attempts found their way here as well. Some of those long-ago stunts might seem inconceivable today, according to Tim Baxter, Oakwood's director of operations and historian. But they were often born of financial necessity. Taylor, a Civil War veteran's widow and retired teacher, dreamed of avoiding poverty and being set for life on speaking circuits. Her aspirations never panned out, and she died in a poor house in Lockport.

"People say, 'These people were crazy,'" Baxter said. "I say they're people in dire situations that made desperate decisions."

Address 763 Portage Road, Niagara Falls, NY 14301, +1 (716) 284-5131, www.oakwoodniagara.org, info@oakwoodniagara.org | Getting there Bus 40, 50, 55, 77 to Portage Road & Cedar Avenue | Hours Mon–Fri 9am–4pm, Sat 10am–1pm | Tip For the best views of the river rapids that challenged so many of the daredevils buried at Oakwood, hike the trails of Whirlpool State Park (Niagara Scenic Parkway, Niagara Falls, www.parks.ny.gov/parks/whirlpool).

96 — The Swan Street Diner

Flap jacks with a side-order of nostalgia

In the heart of Buffalo's Larkinville neighborhood, a restored 1930s diner, trucked in from two hours east, has found a new lease on life – and helped revitalize a community. Customers start filing in the Swan Street Diner's wooden booths and original counter stools early each morning for cups of coffee served in hearty ceramic mugs made in Buffalo. They order from a menu serving elevated diner fare, deciding among tofu scrambles, breakfast tacos, and granola parfaits, or staples like biscuits and gravy, short stacks of flapjacks, and house-made corned beef hash.

You can even brush up on your old-timey diner lingo using the glossary on the back of the menu: "Gimme a raft and checkerboard, and top it with cow paste and motor oil." You've just placed an order for toast and waffles topped with butter and maple syrup. By mid-morning, office workers, college students, and other Buffalonians from all walks of life file into the 50-foot-long diner, which features porcelain ceilings and glass countertops. There's a new buzz in this previously vacant corner of the city.

The restaurant is the brainchild of Buffalo's Zemsky family, who have been gradually redeveloping a formerly fraying stretch of Seneca Street into Buffalo's Larkinville neighborhood, a district filled with offices, breweries, distilleries, and loft apartments. The Zemskys recognized that a missing piece of the Larkinville puzzle was a business that brought in patrons on weekends and during the day, so they began a search for a diner that they could place on the empty corner of Swan and Seneca.

They stumbled upon the 1935 Newark Diner for sale two hours east of Buffalo, purchased it, and brought it back here for restoration. The diner re-opened in 2017 and soon became a neighborhood fixture. This is the perfect place to experience a great American diner and to take a glimpse into Buffalo's future.

Address 700 Swan Street, Buffalo, NY 14210, +1 (716) 768-1823, www.swanstreetdiner.com | Getting there Bus 15 to Swan & Hagerman Streets | Hours Daily 7am–3pm | Tip Sit at the counter and order a cup of homemade soup at the Soup Lady at the 412 Diner, which operates out of an old diner car in North Tonawanda (412 Oliver Street).

97_ The Swannie House

A historic pub and a shipping disaster

Bob Grande will never forget the night he was drinking at The Swannie House, the city's second-oldest pub, when he heard an "unbelievable" noise outside. "I had never heard anything like it before or after," the retired grain scooper recalled. "If you had a plane land outside, it wouldn't have made that much noise." That night was January 21, 1959, when an unmanned lake freighter, the S.S. *Tewksbury*, slammed into the Michigan Avenue bridge just around the corner from the pub.

Behind the original wooden bar at this 1886 waterfront tavern, you'll find an old newspaper article detailing its role on that infamous night. High winds and ice floes knocked the *MacGivray Shiras*, an unmanned vessel, free of its moorings and sent it careening down the Buffalo River. It then slammed into the *Tewksbury*, and the two ghost ships continued down the river on a collision course with the span. The bridge's lift attendants were "tending beers" in the Swannie House before their shift change, *The Buffalo News* reported, and by the time they reached the bridge, it was too late. Grande doesn't remember seeing the attendants inside the bar, but did recall running outside only to find total darkness where the bridge once stood. Daylight revealed a twisted mass of steel beams and wreckage. The blockage in the river sent icy-cold water flooding into the surrounding neighborhood.

Ask the tavern's veteran bartenders about that night, and they'll acknowledge that the bridge attendants' presence there wasn't a surprise. Drinking during a shift was common in those days, when millworkers and longshoremen poured into the pub from nearby docked freighters, grain silos, and warehouses – a bygone era of Buffalo. This small brick pub, with wooden floors and historic photos of tugboats and vintage street maps hanging from its walls, is one of the last vestiges from the waterfront's industrial heyday.

Address 170 Ohio Street, Buffalo, NY 14203, +1 (716) 847-2898, www.facebook.com/ TheSwannieHouse | Getting there Bus 14, 16 to South Park & Michigan Avenues | Hours Mon–Sat 11–4am, Sun 11am–9pm | Tip Raise a glass at another legendary waterfront watering hole nearby, Gene McCarthy's, which opened in 1964 and added a microbrewery in 2014 (73 Hamburg Street, www.genemccarthys.com).

98 The Tara Gift Shoppe
One-stop shop for all things Irish

Along a road lined with street signs written in both English and Gaelic, a family-owned store has carved out a niche as Buffalo's destination for all things Irish. Nearly 10,000 items – from Irish clothes and wares to foods, jewelry, and curiosities – line the Tara Gift Shoppe from floor to ceiling.

This 850-square-foot store is a one-stop shop for Barry's Tea, Connemara Kitchen after dinner mints, Belleek China, O'Neill's Shamrock Shortbread, Hogan's Irish Scone Mix, claddagh earrings and necklaces, and bodhrán drums. Traditional Irish pub music plays in the background as customers browse for shamrock-themed thermal socks, rugby shirts, knit scarves, and Irish caps. The shop is in the heart of South Buffalo's Irish Heritage District, a neighborhood historically settled by Irish immigrants and their descendants that also includes The Buffalo Irish Center, a pub, event hall, and Irish library located in a converted YMCA across the street.

Neither the store nor the neighborhood would be what they are today without the late Mary Heneghan, a former schoolteacher who started the shop back in 1978. In opening the store, Heneghan found a way to turn her lifelong love of Irish culture – both her father and husband emigrated from the Old Sod – into a career. She also served as president of the Irish Center for 25 years, advocating for the neighborhood's Irish heritage until her death in 2022. Her son Tom succeeded her at the shop, and her daughter Mary Kay runs the Rince Ni Tiarna Irish Dance School inside the center.

While Tom Heneghan jokes that his mother "would haunt him" if he ever closed the store, he also can't imagine South Buffalo, where cast iron shamrocks hang from streetlamps on Abbott Road, without it. "You don't want to forget where you came from," Heneghan says, "Or you won't know where you're going."

Address 250 Abbott Road, Buffalo, NY 14220, +1 (716) 825-6700, www.taragiftshoppe.com, taragiftshoppe@gmail.com | Getting there Bus 14 to Abbott Road & Mumford Street | Hours Mon–Thu, Sat 10am–4pm, Fri 10am–6pm | Tip Wander across the street after your shopping spree for a freshly poured Guinness at Buffalo Irish Center's pub (245 Abbott Road, www.buffaloirishcenter.com).

99 Thomas Pafk Design
Fine woodworking in the Roycroft tradition

Each morning, Thomas Pafk carves, chisels, and hammers inside his workshop, transforming some of the 10,000 wooden blocks and boards lining his walls into his next piece. The scent of freshly cut cherry, oak, and maple greets visitors when they walk into Pafk's woodworking studio along a country road on the outskirts of East Aurora.

Pafk often spends days, weeks, or even months creating his next piece, from picture frames and candlesticks to cabinets, dressers, and entire dining sets. He sells his work inside a small, wooden, former 1850 schoolhouse at the front of the property known as the Schoolhouse Gallery, a cooperative run by Pafk and other artisans. Pafk's work carries on a tradition of craftsmanship in East Aurora that dates back generations. "You know the saying, 'Keep Austin Weird'? We like to say, 'Keep East Aurora quirky,'" Pafk said. "Everyone does their own thing. This has always been a very creative, artist-driven town."

That spirit of creativity started more than a century ago, when entrepreneur Elbert Hubbard founded the Roycroft Campus, a colony of printers, metalsmiths, and woodworkers who launched the American Arts and Crafts Movement. The campus produced handcrafted books, metalwork, and furniture until its bankruptcy in the Great Depression. Decades later, a group of artisans revived that era's design standards by launching the Roycroft Renaissance, a juried collective that Pafk joined more than 25 years ago.

Pafk considers his work to be "Roycroft redesigned," a modern take on the original Roycroft furniture. He carves a double-R into every piece he creates – the Roycroft Renaissance mark of quality – and is one of the only local artisans in the group to operate an open studio. Visiting Pafk's workshop is one of the best ways to experience East Aurora's handcrafted legacy, alive and well today, and to see a master artisan at work.

Address 1054 Olean Road, East Aurora, NY 14052, +1 (716) 655-3229, www.thomaspafkdesign.com, thomas@thomaspafkdesign.com | **Getting there** By car, take 400 S to US-20A toward East Aurora to NY-16 S to Olean Road | **Hours** Mon – Sat 10am – 4pm | **Tip** Stop in at Bar-Bill Tavern, where staff hand-brush a variety of homemade sauces onto every plate of wings served (185 Main Street, East Aurora, www.barbill.com).

100 Tifft Nature Preserve

A natural oasis in the heart of the city

Just a few minutes south of downtown, deer graze against the backdrop of grain silos, and hikers explore miles of trails in a nature preserve reclaimed from pollution and industry.

The 264-acre Tifft Nature Preserve is a natural oasis in the heart of the city. It's almost inconceivable that this quiet, serene park was once the site of a city dump and a shipping center. River otters, beavers, and blue-spotted salamanders thrive along an unusually shaped lake that was built as a canal teeming with lake freighters. You can climb atop the "Mounds," a grassy, hilly covered landfill, for sweeping views of Lake Erie and the city skyline.

And while you're hiking the preserve's five miles of forest trails, you might stumble upon an occasional railroad tie – a reminder of the property's industrial past. The grinding noise of boxcars and garbage trucks has been replaced by the chirping of more than 200 species of birds who call the preserve home throughout the year. They fly through the centuries-old cattail marsh, the only portion of the preserve that remains intact from Buffalo's earliest days. "Very quickly, you tune out the road noise and forget that you're in the city of Buffalo," said Tifft's director Meghan Dye. "It's such an escape."

A half-century ago, the area long known as Tifft Farm for the cattle barns that once operated there was far less of a refuge. The shipping area had been abandoned, and the property had become a dumping ground. When the city chose the area to store its solid waste in the 1970s, a group of activists lobbied to have the new landfill capped and converted into one of the country's first urban nature preserves. The site represents one of Buffalo's first success stories to convert formerly industrial land into an enjoyable public space. After generations of misuse and abandonment, nature has found a way to thrive here once again.

Address 1200 Fuhrmann Boulevard, Buffalo, NY 14203, +1 (716) 825-6397, www.tifft.org | **Getting there** Bus 42 to Fuhrmann Boulevard & Tifft Farms | **Hours** Daily dawn–dusk; Education Center Wed–Sun 10am–4pm | **Tip** Carved from the estate of Dr. Victor Reinstein, the Reinstein Woods Nature Preserve is a 244-acre greenspace with miles of trails winding their way through forests and wetlands (93 Honorine Drive, Depew, http://www.reinsteinwoods.org).

101 UB's Special Collections

James Joyce's home away from home

James Joyce never set foot in Buffalo, and yet the largest collection of works from the acclaimed Irish author resides here, tucked away inside a University at Buffalo (UB) library. UB's Poetry Collection on its North Campus houses more than 10,000 pages of Joyce's work and has become a destination for self-professed "Joyceans" from around the world.

The collection includes his notes and scribbles in journals that shed light on his writing process for books like *Finnegan's Wake*, and other ephemera, like his cane, glasses, and passport. UB also has one of the first copies of *Ulysses* that features a handwritten note to Sylvia Beach, owner of the Paris bookstore Shakespeare & Company. And there's even a copy of *A Farewell to Arms*, which Ernest Hemingway gifted his friend Joyce – with all the swear words that the editors had removed scribbled back in by the author.

Buffalo may seem like an unusual destination for all things James Joyce, yet the collection speaks to UB's ambition to become one of the world's greatest collectors of rare and special books. Several years after Joyce's death in 1941, UB professor Oscar Silverman attended a Joyce exposition in Paris in 1949, and ultimately the items from that event were gifted to UB. The collection grew over subsequent decades, including acquisitions from Beach herself, and continues to expand today.

"We have, to the best of our ability, everything by and about Joyce that has ever been written," said James Maynard, PhD, coordinator of the Rare and Special Books Collection. "The archive helps flesh him out as a living person." Seeing the Joyce Collection is currently by appointment only, and the library staff assembles the "greatest hits" for viewing upon request. UB is planning a permanent exhibition of Joyce's work on its South Campus, which will increase the visibility of this extraordinary collection.

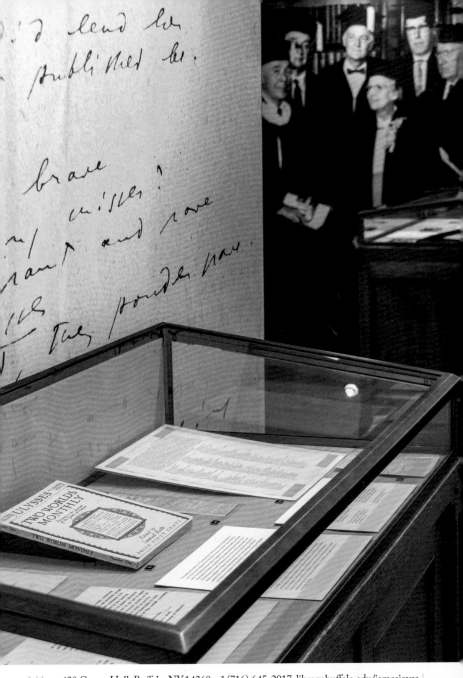

Address 420 Capen Hall, Buffalo, NY 14260, +1 (716) 645-2917, library.buffalo.edu/jamesjoyce |
Getting there Bus 35, 44 to Flint Circle | Hours By appointment only | Tip The Karpeles
Manuscript Library Museum has a series of literary, historical, and scientific manuscripts on display
inside a beautiful former church (220 North Street, www.karpeles.com/visit/buffalo-new-york).

102__Underground Railroad Museum

Retrace the harrowing journeys of freedom seekers

"The shores of Canada had been tantalizing my longing gaze for some days, and … I made a strike for freedom!" recalled Nancy Berry, a formerly enslaved person who crossed the Niagara River just below the falls, in Lucy Delaney's 1890 book, *From the Darkness Cometh the Light, or Struggles for Freedom*. "Hastily I embarked, and as the boat stole away into the misty twilight and among crushing fields of ice, … I felt the warmth of freedom as I reached the Canada shore."

In the years leading up to the Civil War, Berry and thousands of other enslaved people completed their journey to freedom through Niagara Falls. The Niagara Falls Underground Railroad Heritage Center, which opened in 2018 inside a converted 1863 Customs House near the river, recounts the stories of freedom seekers like Berry, who built a new life across the border – and of local abolitionists who risked everything to protect them.

The museum's exhibit rooms replicate key Niagara Falls stops along the famed secret network. You'll cross a model of a wooden suspension bridge to Canada that once stood outside the museum, and walk through the recreated dining room of the long-demolished Cataract House, where free African American waiters worked undercover to free those people enslaved by the hotel's Southern guests.

Exhibits highlight once-forgotten figures in the region's Underground Railroad history. John Morrison, the African American head waiter of the Cataract House, rowed freedom seekers to Canada at night after his shift. Patrick Sneed, a formerly enslaved person, successfully defended his freedom against his enslaver's fraudulent claims in a Buffalo courthouse. The center's painstaking efforts to share these narratives of heroism and resilience will ensure they live on for generations to come.

Address 825 Depot Avenue W, Niagara Falls, NY 14305, +1 (716) 300-8477,
www.niagarafallsundergroundrailroad.org, info@niagarafallsundergroundrailroad.org |
Getting there Bus 52 to Main Street & Depot Avenue | Hours Wed–Sun 10am–5pm |
Tip Discover more Underground Railroad History along the Niagara River at Buffalo's
Broderick Park, a designated Network to Freedom Site by the National Park Service
(1170 Niagara Street, www.visitbuffaloniagara.com/businesses/broderick-park).

103 Undergrounds Coffeehouse

A funeral home turned café

It wasn't always Sara Heidinger's intention to open a coffeehouse inside a former funeral home. But when opportunity presented itself, she decided to think outside the box.

Undergrounds Coffeehouse posts "calling hours" instead of business hours on its entrance and sells T-shirts that tout its slogan, "Start your day before it ends." Customers grab cream and sugar at the "creamation" station and order sandwiches named after late, famous Buffalonians like Tim Russert and Rick James. The café's bathroom has a planter on its floor filled with ceramic skulls donated by customers and a wall mural featuring two dancing skeletons.

Frequent patrons buy into the Mug Club, which includes a customized, hand-thrown mug with the picture of a famous deceased figure they'd most like to have coffee with. The shop sells bags of "white light" roasted coffee named after famous women, like the "Thank you for Being a Blend" variety that honors the stars of The Golden Girls. And early birds just might find a "mourning" special on the menu. "We just liked the idea of celebrating what the space used to be," Heidinger said. "In the death of the funeral home was the birth of the coffee shop."

Heidinger grew up in the neighborhood and saw an opportunity to provide the Old First Ward with its first coffeehouse after she moved back from New York City. The former Peter K. Leslie Funeral Home proved to be the perfect fit for a new community gathering space. Undergrounds roasts its own beans weekly and prides itself on accessible options, like its "just a cup," which Heidinger designed for her father who had no interest in lattes or macchiatos. For Heidinger, this funeral home-turned-café presented an opportunity to honor "those who came before us," and celebrate life alongside death – all over a cup of great coffee.

Address 580 South Park Avenue, Buffalo, NY 14210, +1 (716) 240-9923,
www.undergroundscoffeebuffalo.com | Getting there Bus 14, 16, 18 to South Park
Avenue & Hamburg Street | Hours Mon–Fri 6am–2pm, Sat & Sun 7:30am–3pm |
Tip Just down Hamburg Street is another adaptive reuse project, The Barrel Factory,
a brewery, distillery, and kayak outfitter (65 Vandalia Street, www.barrelfactory.com).

104 The Van Horn Mansion
A centuries-old home full of spirits

Back when the old Van Horn Mansion sat vacant, passing motorists sometimes noticed a woman with long, flowing hair peeking out from a bedroom window of the otherwise empty house.

Spooky experiences frightened many of the volunteers who first stepped inside the home four decades ago to begin restoring it. Some vowed never to return. Even today, visitors to the 200-year-old mansion, one of the oldest homes in Western New York, occasionally hear footsteps where no one is walking and smell the faint aroma of flowers and cigars. Janice Wiegley, tour guide and president of the Town of Newfane Historical Society, Inc., experienced an invisible force yanking on strands of her hair while she was leading a group through the same upstairs bedroom. "I wouldn't say I believe [in ghosts]; I wouldn't say I disbelieve," she said. "But I can't explain some of the things that happened to me here."

Historians attribute the paranormal activity to the spirit of Malinda Van Horn, one of the earliest residents of the property who may have died due to complications from childbirth at the age of 21. For decades, her headstone lay in storage at the site until a search by cadaver dogs in the 1990s revealed human remains that were likely hers near the house. With her headstone and gravesite reunited, Malinda's spirit seems to have settled down.

Since then, the Historical Society has magnificently restored the 6-bedroom, 3-bathroom home that was once owned by one of Niagara County's most prominent families before suffering years of abandonment and neglect. Visitors can tour the refurbished mansion, which is decorated with Victorian-era furniture largely donated by town residents. This house museum offers the rare opportunity to learn how generations of one local family once lived – and perhaps even a chance to encounter the spirit of one Van Horn who may have never left.

Address 2159 Lockport Olcott Road, Burt, NY 14028, +1 (716) 778-7197, www.vanhornmansion.com | Getting there By car, take Route 78 N towards Burt to the destination on the right. | Hours See website for tour schedule | Tip Cap off a day of hauntings with dinner at The Red Coach Inn, a 100-year-old hotel in downtown Niagara Falls that is believed to be filled with spirits, including a ghostly bride (2 Buffalo Avenue, Niagara Falls, www.redcoach.com/restaurant).

105__ Vidler's 5 & 10

A nostalgic five-and-dime for modern times

"If Vidler's doesn't have it, you don't need it," third-generation co-owner Don Vidler says about the sprawling five-and-dime store started by his grandfather nearly a century ago. Vidler's 5 and 10, one of the last retailers of its kind left in the United States, features more than 75,000 items spread across two floors and four interconnected storefronts.

Along its original, creaking hardwood floors, you'll find an old-fashioned candy counter that features Charleston Chews, Necco Wafers, Lemonheads, and other confections. A nearby novelty section sells oddities, like a yodeling pickle, Captain Kirk finger puppets, and a "stool sample" (a miniature wooden stool placed within a vial). This is a one-stop shop for bacon-flavored soda, sugar cube tongs, harmonicas, tin kazoos, cowgirl lip balm, Ass Blaster brand hot sauce, and Magic 8 Balls.

Vidler's 12 different departments include a card shop, souvenir shop, housewares section, and a year-round Christmas boutique, not to mention Sandy the Mare Horse, a coin-operated steed that children have ridden since 1963. The store's red-and-white awnings and its Vidler on the Roof – a bespectacled, smiling, eight-foot-tall likeness of Don's late father Ed – make it a can't-miss East Aurora landmark.

"We're the antithesis of Wal-Mart or online shopping," Don Vidler adds. "It's very Andy of Mayberry in here." Don's grandfather first opened the original 18-foot-wide and 50-foot-long store back in 1930. Ed and his brother Bob had the foresight in the 1970s to market the store's nostalgia and expand its inventory to include more novelty merchandise.

As other five-and-dimes folded across the country, Vidler's endured and expanded, attracting tour buses and other far-flung visitors. There simply aren't many places left like Vidler's, a multigenerational, family-owned store that embodies a bygone era of American retailing.

Address 676-694 Main Street, East Aurora, NY 14052, +1 (716) 652-0481, www.vidlers5and10.com | Getting there Bus 70 to East Main & Church Streets | Hours Mon – Sat 9am – 6pm, Sun 11am – 5pm | Tip The Marilla Country Store may be the region's oldest shop, dating back to 1851 (1673 Two Rod Road, Marilla, www.marillacountrystore.com).

106 __ Viola's Submarine Shop

Niagara Falls' signature sandwich

Don't mistake the steak and cheese sub served at Viola's with its better-known cousin, the Philly cheesesteak. They're separate and distinct sandwiches. Niagara Falls' signature sandwich features pieces of ribeye placed on a flat grill and covered with a slice of American cheese, then topped with Viola's "everything": lettuce, diced tomato and onion, oil, and a house seasoning. It's not quite like any other steak sandwich, including the cheesesteak, which typically has more finely chopped beef covered in Cheez Whiz and no lettuce or tomato. "You can't go outside of Western New York and find a sub like ours," co-owner Peter Tardibuono said. "We're going to make it the way we've always done it. Everything we do, we try to keep it consistent."

Peter's late father Joseph Tardibuono and uncle Otto Viola first conceived of the sandwich made with fresh ribeye when they opened their first shop in 1958 in the city's Italian neighborhood. A second location soon followed on Military Road. Viola's serves a host of other subs with Italian cold cuts, like capicola, pepperoni, and mortadella, but it was the steak and cheese that took off and became more than two-thirds of its sales.

Little has changed here through the decades. The same Canadian bakery has delivered fresh sub rolls daily for 50 years, and staff hand-cut the ribeye every morning just as Joseph and Otto once did. Peter Tardibuono started working here in 1980 when he was 17 and still occasionally grills in the shop he now co-owns.

The tucked-away Elmwood Avenue outlet is a true throwback and pilgrimage-worthy. Vintage signs advertising Vernors Ginger Ale and *the best sandwich in town* flank its exterior, while an antique cash register sits behind the counter inside. One bite of the steak and cheese will reveal why this store is often the first stop for returning expatriates looking for a taste of home.

Address **Address** 1717 Elmwood Avenue, Niagara Falls, NY 14301, +1 (716) 282-7094, facebook.com/violassubmarineshop | **Getting there** Bus 55 to Pine Avenue & 17th Street, then walk five minutes north on W Market Street to Elmwood Avenue | **Hours** Mon–Sat 10:30am–10pm, Sun noon–7pm | **Tip** Enjoy a slice from DiCamillo Bakery, which has been making pizza since opening in 1920 (811 Linwood Avenue, Niagara Falls, www.dicamillobakery.com).

107 Whitworth Planetarium

Cutting-edge center for stargazing

Stepping inside the Whitworth Ferguson Planetarium is like climbing aboard "a spaceship that allows you to ride anywhere in the Universe," according to director Kevin Williams.

This is not your grandfather's planetarium. The 48-seat facility, which opened in 2021 inside Buffalo State University's Science & Mathematics Complex, features a state-of-the-art star projector, digital displays, and laser-light rock shows. On any given night, guests staring up at the planetarium's 35-foot-wide, 360-degree dome might discover an up-close view of the swirling Milky Way Galaxy or the topography of Mars.

You can experience the rage and fury of a solar superstorm through an immersive film, or watch lasers dart across the room set to the music of Pink Floyd, Rush, and Queen. Some shows begin by displaying the handful of stars typically viewed over Buffalo, then expanding into thousands of points of light and constellations that would be visible without light pollution. "In some ways, we're using cutting edge technology to connect people to the sky like they saw thousands of years ago," says Williams.

Buffalo State has had a planetarium since the 1960s, back when nearly every public college across the state received one during the US' effort to win the Space Race against the Soviet Union. The original burned to the ground in the 1970s and was then replaced in the early 1980s. (Look for the vintage star projector from this planetarium right outside the current one.)

The newest facility, which was completed during a recent college expansion, features a massive sphere plated with tiles tilted at 23 degrees, the same angle on which the Earth rests on its axis. Students walking outside can see the sphere through floor-to-ceiling windows. This planetarium is one of Buffalo's greatest hidden gems: a portal to the heavens tucked away in the middle of a college campus.

Address 1300 Elmwood Avenue, Science & Mathematics Complex 150, Buffalo, NY 14222, +1 (716) 878-4911, planetarium.buffalostate.edu, planetarium@buffalostate.edu | Getting there Bus 3 to Grant Street & Buffalo State College, follow campus signs to planetarium | Hours Check website for show schedule | Tip Look up at the star-filled sky away from the light pollution of the city at the Beaver Meadow Audubon Center in North Java, where the Buffalo Astronomical Association hosts regular public viewing nights in the summer and fall (1610 Welch Road, Java, www.facebook.com/BuffaloAstronomy).

108 The Winery at Marjim Manor

Sipping with the spirits

What's the difference between a wine and a spirit? ask the T-shirts sold at The Winery at Marjim Manor. *Wine is what we serve here. Spirits are who you meet.* Visitors have encountered many spirits at this 19th-century estate-turned-winery along the shores of Lake Ontario.

Sometimes they see longtime resident Dr. Charles Ring, who died inside the house more than a century ago, staring out at them from a front-room mirror. Other times, an apparition of Shubal Merritt appears, the man who built the house and was rumored for generations to have accidentally murdered his son here. Estelle Morse, a subsequent owner who shared that rumor with the *New York World Magazine* in 1908 and popularized the estate's reputation as the "Hoodoo House," occasionally materializes at the front door, according to current owner Margo Sue Bittner. And other encounters abound at this 25-room manor situated on 200 rural acres, from slamming doors to digital cameras simultaneously shutting off at a wedding, and even an occasional vision of the Sisters of St. Joseph, who once used the property as a retreat house.

Bittner pours out all these stories and more alongside glasses of the fruit-flavored wine in which Marjim Manor specializes. Her husband Jim owns a series of nearby fruit orchards that the winery sources for more than three-dozen flavors, like the "Thursday Afternoon at 3," a peach and grape blend named for the moment Dr. Ring died here, and "Shubal's Sunset," a blush wine in honor of Shubal Merritt.

Since purchasing the property in 2004, Bittner has also discovered that Merritt did not, in fact, kill his son. The spirits who do appear here appreciate her sharing the truth, she said, and simply want to share in the good memories created here. "Our job is to pour wine and tell ghost stories," she said. "Can anything be more fun than that?"

Address 7171 E Lake Road, Appleton, NY 14008, +1 (716) 778-7001, www.marjimmanor.com |
Getting there By car, take Route 78 N to Route 18 E | Hours Mon–Sat 10am–6pm,
Sun noon–6pm | Tip Pair your wine with a bag of freshly popped popcorn from Bye's Popcorn, a
roadside stand in nearby Olcott since 1923 (1667 Lockport-Olcott Road, www.byespopcorn.net).

109 Winter Cave of the Winds
Frozen fun at the falls

Hearty souls brave frigid conditions each winter at the base of the Niagara Gorge to witness a spectacle unlike anywhere else in the world: Niagara Falls encased in ice. The Cave of the Winds has been one of Niagara Falls' most popular experiences for generations, bringing visitors down a 17-story, 175-foot elevator shaft to explore the base of the Bridal Veil Falls on a series of wooden decks. Several years ago, New York State Parks expanded this attraction from seasonal to year-round, providing visitors with an up-close view of the icy cataract in the wintertime.

As the temperatures plunge, coatings of frozen mist and snow accumulate on the hundreds of rocks at the base of the falls like layers of an ice cream cake. They create glacial-like formations up to 50 feet high and surround the 75,000 gallons of roaring water flowing over the American and Bridal Veil Falls each second. The frozen mist settles on everything in its path, from tree boughs to the rocky walls of the gorge. On sunny winter afternoons, rainbows form across the icy, misty landscape. Colder winters with frequent blasts of frigid air create an especially spectacular scene.

A winter visit to the Cave of the Winds begins with the elevator ride down the Niagara Gorge that leads to a viewing area at the base of the falls, which is coated in ice on below-freezing days and can be slippery. The swirling, frozen mist carried by the winds can also cover winter coats and eyelashes, so come prepared for the wintry elements – and for an unforgettable, once-in-a-lifetime memory.

This attraction originally derived its name from a long-destroyed rocky overhang that created a cavern behind the Bridal Veil Falls, known as "Aeolus' Cave," after the Greek god of the winds. While throngs of crowds flock here every summer, those in the know bundle up and endure the cold for an unrivaled outdoor experience.

Address Goat Island Road, Niagara Falls, NY 14202, +1 (716) 560-8170, www.niagarafallsstatepark.com | **Getting there** Bus 7, 40, 50 to Rainbow Boulevard and First Street, continue on First Street over the Niagara River to Goat Island Road | **Hours** See website for seasonal tour schedule | **Tip** Discover another unique winter experience in Buffalo by riding the Ice Bikes of Buffalo, which were the first of their kind in North America when they debuted in 2014 (44 Prime Street, www.waterbikesofbuffalo.com/ice-bikes).

110 WNY's Book Arts Center
Keeping the art of letterpress alive

Nestled among downtown's modern offices, tech hubs, and co-working spaces, the Western New York Book Arts Center keeps the lost art of letterpress alive. This basement studio filled with printing presses is as much an exhibit dedicated to the history of printing in Buffalo as it is a working studio.

Member artisans use one of several printing presses, paper cutters, and other equipment – some of which dates back to the late 19th century – to create greeting cards, fine art prints, wedding invitations, band posters, and other printed materials. They can choose from thousands of antique "cuts," the clip art of yesteryear that print shops across Buffalo once used, to complete their designs. The center sells its members' creations in a small shop upstairs, and you can also sign up for workshops and tours. "It's one thing to go to a museum, but it's another to go see old museum things that are still in use," Education Director Rosemary Williams said. "It's cool to work with something with historical roots to it and make something new … without understanding letterpress, you lose how things used to be made."

A studio like this is particularly possible in an older, legacy city like Buffalo, where print shops once operated on nearly every corner, Williams noted. The medium's demise left unused printing equipment and cuts throughout the city, some of which the center procured through donations and purchases after it opened in 2006. The studio features dozens of cuts that once served as logos and advertisements for long-shuttered Buffalo businesses like, The Sample Shop, Michael's House of Steaks, Sattler's Department Store, Bellevue Fashion Shops, and Ulbrich's Bookstores. Visiting here provides a chance to relive a medium that Buffalo and its businesses once depended on – and an opportunity to see a new generation bring that art form back to life.

Address 468 Washington Street, Buffalo, NY 14203, +1 (716) 348-1430, www.wnybookarts.org, curious@wnybookarts.org | Getting there Metro Rail to Evans Bank @ Lafayette Square; bus 6, 14, 16, 24 to Washington & Mohawk Streets | Hours Wed – Fri 11am – 5pm, Sat 10am – 2pm | Tip Hone your writing skills upstairs at the Just Buffalo Literary Center, which offers writing workshops for teenagers and adults (468 Washington Street, 2nd floor, www.justbuffalo.org).

111 Wright's Gas Station

A long-shelved design stunningly comes to life

James Sandoro relishes the "holy cow" moment guests have inside his museum when they first discover the massive replica of a gas station designed by Frank Lloyd Wright. The filling station, which anchors the Buffalo Transportation Pierce-Arrow Museum, is one of only two in the world designed by the architect.

Wright called his 1927 proposal for the corner of Michigan and Cherry Streets in downtown Buffalo "an ornament to the pavement" and spared no detail – or expense – in his blueprints. The station features 60-foot-tall totem poles that support a sign advertising Tydol gas, gravity-fed pumps, a sitting room with a fireplace and couch, a sleeping room for the attendant, a small store, and separate bathrooms for men and women. Sandoro even outfitted the station with period furnishings, including a sanitary napkin dispenser and a public health advertisement warning against the dangers of syphilis.

Wright's gas station may have looked great on paper, but its construction proved to be cost-prohibitive, and his unrealized sketches sat tucked away at his Taliesin West compound in Phoenix, Arizona for decades. Sandoro, who has spent most of his life collecting cars and auto memorabilia, first discovered the sketches while doing research years ago and sought to bring the design to life in the city it was intended to be. "It's incomplete Buffalo history, so why not complete it?" Sandoro said.

He assembled a team that took more than two and a half years to build the station, which complements the museum's thousands of pieces of automobile memorabilia and dozens of Buffalo-made cars. The exhibit opened in 2014, some 87 years after Wright first designed it and 55 years after his death. Sandoro enclosed the station to protect it from Buffalo's harsh winters, ensuring that a design that almost never saw the light of day will be preserved for posterity.

Address 263 Michigan Avenue, Buffalo, NY 14203, +1 (716) 853-0084, www.pierce-arrow.com |
Getting there Bus 15 to Swan Street & Michigan Avenue | Hours Fri & Sat 11am – 4pm |
Tip Discover another posthumously designed building by Frank Lloyd Wright, the Fontana
Boathouse, which was completed in 2007 (1 Rotary Row, www.franklloydwrightboathouse.com).

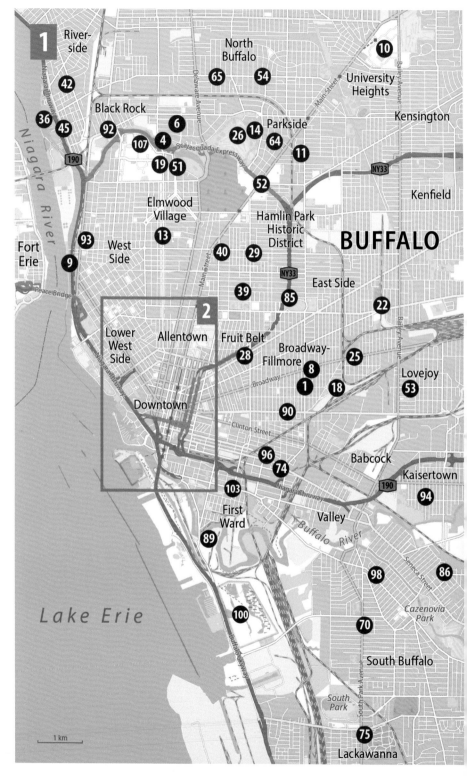

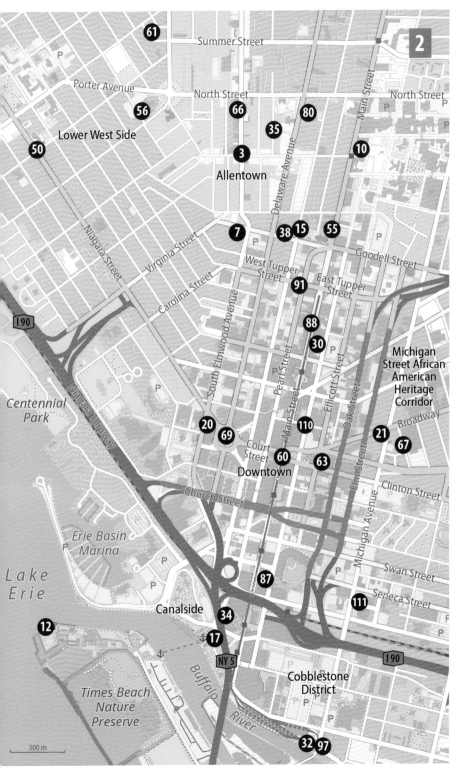

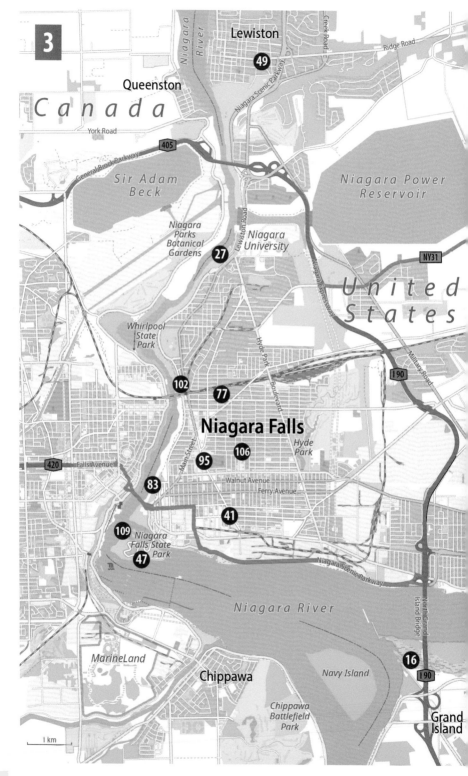

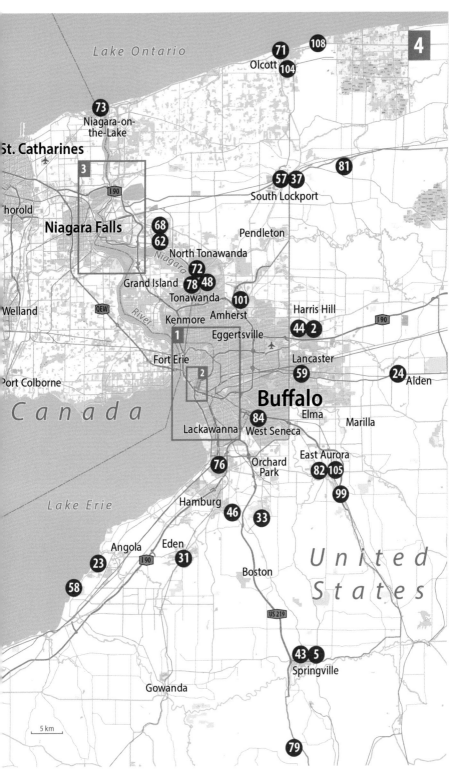

Elizabeth Lenell-Davies,
Anita Genua, Claire Davenport
111 Places in Toronto
That You Must Not Miss
ISBN 978-3-7408-0257-8

Jennifer Bain, Liz Beddall
111 Places in Ottawa
That You Must Not Miss
ISBN 978-3-7408-1388-8

Jo-Anne Elikann, Susan Lusk
111 Places in New York
That You Must Not Miss
ISBN 978-3-7408-1888-3

Kim Windyka, Heather Kapplow,
Alyssa Wood
111 Places in Boston
That You Must Not Miss
ISBN 978-3-7408-1558-5

Andréa Seiger, John Dean
111 Places in Washington
That You Must Not Miss
ISBN 978-3-7408-1890-6

Brandon Schultz, Lucy Baber
111 Places in Philadelphia
That You Must Not Miss
ISBN 978-3-7408-1376-5

Allison Robicelli, John Dean
111 Places in Baltimore
That You Must Not Miss
ISBN 978-3-7408-1696-4

Michelle Madden, Janet McMillan
111 Places in Milwaukee
That You Must Not Miss
ISBN 978-3-7408-1643-8

Sandra Gurvis, Mitch Geiser
111 Places in Columbus
That You Must Not Miss
ISBN 978-3-7408-0600-2

Photo Credits

All photos by Jesse Pitzler except:

Explore & More (ch. 34): Photo by Joe Cascio

Lake Erie's Ice Volcanoes (ch. 58): Photos courtesy
of Matthew Nusstein

The Lancaster Opera House (ch. 59): Angela Doll Photography

Our Lady of Victory Basilica (ch. 76):
OLV National Shrine & Basilica

Stitch Buffalo (ch. 94): Michael Mandolfo

The Van Horn Mansion (ch. 104): Rich Leader, RL-Films.com

Winter Cave of the Winds (ch. 109): NYS Parks

Art Credits

Burchfield Penney Art Center (ch. 19):
Charles E. Burchfield's Gardenville Studio
is on permanent view at the Burchfield Penney Art Center.

The Colored Musicians Museum (ch. 21):
Painting on the front of the building done by Herbie Small

The Freedom Wall, 2017 (ch. 40): by John Baker,
Julia Bottoms, Chuck Tingley, and Edreys Wajed – on
the corner of Michigan Avenue and East Ferry Street

Hispanic Heritage Mural (ch. 50): Betsy Z. Casañas

Working People (ch. 52): Photographs by Milton Rogovin

The Martin House (ch. 65):
Courtesy Frank Lloyd Wright's Martin House

Our Lady of Victory Basilica (ch. 76):
OLV National Shrine & Basilica

The Prophet Isaiah House (ch. 78):
Artwork by Prophet Isaiah Robertson, with permission
of Niagara Falls National Heritage Area

Undergrounds Coffee Mural (ch. 104): Artist Nicole Cherry

Whitworth Planetarium (ch. 107): Whitworth Ferguson
Planetarium, SUNY Buffalo State University 2023

Special gratitude to travel writer and friend Jennifer Bain, who introduced me to this series during the pandemic and connected me to the 111 Places team to draft a proposal. Jesse Pitzler: your extraordinary talent as a photographer and unique lens brought each of these chapters to life. To my partner Mel, thank you for your kindness and patience as the book came together during the time where we decided to spend the rest of our lives together. And to my mother Ann, whose keen proofreading eye helped immensely in the final stages. Thanks as well to The Buffalo History Museum and Library Director Cynthia Van Ness, whose assistance enriched so many of these chapters with a historical perspective. To my editor Karen Sciger, it was a pleasure working with you to create a guide for a city we both love. And to the dozens of friends, acquaintances, and current and former colleagues who offered suggestions and ideas over cups of coffee, lunch, driving tours, and drinks. Finally, behind nearly every one of the 111 places was a person who took time out of their day to chat about what makes that spot exceptional. Thank you for believing in this book.

Brian Hayden

Taking photographs of so many various locations, chapters, and subjects requires guidance and support from many people and places. I am incredibly grateful to my wife Gabrielle, for encouraging and challenging me to take on this project, and for accompanying me on many photo shoots. Her support and companionship made this project possible. I am also grateful for the love and support of my family throughout this journey. To my friend Maggie who never did get a chance to visit, but was with me in spirit for every photo that I took. I would like to thank our author Brian, whose mastery of Buffalo's history and personal experience of this amazing area brought this book to life. Additionally, I am grateful to my editor Karen, who continuously helped us work out obstacles and kept us on target. Finally, I would like to thank the great people and places who allowed me to capture their stories and share them through these photographs. Thank you all for being a part of this with me.

Jesse Pitzler

Brian Hayden is a lifelong Buffalonian with a passion for travel and storytelling. His background in journalism, history, and destination marketing – including roles at Visit Buffalo Niagara and The Buffalo History Museum – have given him a rich perspective on all that Buffalo, Niagara Falls and Western New York have to offer.

Jesse Pitzler started his journey as a photographer and cinematographer in Seattle after separating from the Marine Corps. He moved to Austin in 2017 to finish his education, and he completed his first book *111 Places in Austin That You Must Not Miss*. He has traveled across the United States, creating beautiful visuals for various mediums. Now living near Buffalo, Jesse is continuing to share his perspective in Western New York, one photo at a time.